IDENTITY'S LAST SECRET

Praise for Identity's Last Secret

In this unique fusion of poetry, painting, and philosophy, mantra, yantra and tantra, Makarand R. Paranjape attempts "bridging the human and the divine." A compelling read.

—Abhay K., poet, translator, and India's ambassador to Madagascar

This is obviously an interesting and ambitious book in the way it consciously embraces varied genres, in the sweep and breadth of its concerns. And then there is the central theme of romantic love—and I liked the fact that this is unabashedly centre-stage, and invoked in all its particularity and its more generic archetypal aspects. And what I shall carry away with me, in particular, are those haunting lines, quietly arrived at: "Identity's last secret/could never be known—or even if known, it could never be told/he was not merely loved, he was beloved—and he was not alone."

There are two ways to read this book. One, as a self-conscious, scholarly literary exercise, intent on proving scale and versatility in its ability to straddle verse, literary theory, myth and metaphysics. But it is also possible to read it as an urgent somewhat vulnerable attempt to piece a ravaged history into a semblance of wholeness and sanity. By the time I reached the last section—which is also, to my mind, the strongest—I found myself moved by a depth of insight that seemed to me not just born of a desire for tidy conclusions and immaculate theories. I saw the mythic retelling more as a human acknowledgement of confusion and failure, as a renewed pledge, tattered but resilient, to confront the terror and uncertainty of living a life "utterly disarmed by love."

—Arundhati Subramaniam, Sahitya Akademi award-winning poet and writer

Makarand R. Paranjape's writing is a treasure that must be discovered and savoured, just as if we were listening to music or poetry. Through well sculpted words and architectonic constructions Makarand lays bare his mind, and we who want to enter it, must do so as devotees enter a temple. In his writings we find sheer sensuality and serene spirituality, places of comfort and spaces of rest, but equally there are uphill tracts that we must climb and winding roads that we must traverse. His writing invites us to look not only at the world outside but at the universe within us, and we return to it again and again, to dip ourselves in the river of beauty that he creates.

—Harsha V. Dehejia, Indo-Canadian medical practitioner, author, Indologist, and exponent of the Krishna arts and aesthetics

Identity's Last Secret has to be seen as a "book" that surpasses all traditional genres. It is avant-garde and traditional at the same time, and that is where its magic comes from: the deft weaving of prose and poetry, of figure and space, of time and self, of adolescent love and the ultimate search for the self that has been central to Indian poetry and philosophy right from the early days of the Rigveda and Bhakti and Sufi poetry. The lover and the devotee, the seeker and the sought, the self and the other merge into each other here, and the outcome is an Upanishadic realisation of that invisible, intractable, unteachable higher self—a realisation that can never be complete as long as we remain what we are with our limited sensory perception and even more limited intelligence. The weave of this book, intertextual and intergeneric, is as important as what it says: the text and the texture enrich and complement each other. Certainly, a breakthrough work that addresses the past and present and the timeless self.

—K. Satchidanandan, one of India's greatest living poets, and award-winning, internationally acclaimed author, critic, professor, and former Secretary, Sahitya Akademi (India's National Academy of Letters).

Humane and congenial, written with verve and creative fervour, *Identity's Last Secret* by Makarand R. Paranjape is rich with vibrant imagery. Each section of the book displays an assemblage of visual and literary elements. His poems and literary passages are lavishly illustrated with Tantric, esoteric codes such as mantra, visual symbols, yantra, mandala, and sacred icons.

Paranjape creates his very own sensorial style of expression closer to Chitra-kavya "picture poems." The book is more than a mosaic of verbal and visual symbols. The subtext that runs through it charts the internal journey of the divided-self yearning for spiritual wholeness. To my surprise and delight, Paranjape finds his liberation in the transforming experience of "harmonious reciprocity of male and female unity", which is, indeed, the ultimate goal of Tantric Sadhana.

—Madhu Khanna, Former Director, Centre for the Study of Comparative Religion & Civilizations, Jamia Millia Islamia, Professor of Indic Religions, founding-president, Tantra Foundation, New Delhi

It is a pleasure reading this myriad-hued work by Makarand R. Paranjape, one of India's foremost intellectuals. His chiselled creativity, profound and well-honed critical thinking, and the capacity to "play" with the text, at a deep level, are all manifest in a work which is in a genre all its own.

—Oopalee Operajita, Distinguished Fellow, Carnegie Mellon University; choreographer and classical artist

I have rarely met a person who "glows" his mind as radiantly and refreshingly as Makarand R. Paranjape. He is a cultural critic, philosopher, spiritual seeker and poet, all rolled disarmingly into one.

Reading *Identity's Last Secret* is like being swept away by a tsunami of conflicting emotions teeming with agony and pain, joy and love, and spiritual highs tinged with eroticism.

This is poetry that honours the masculine and feminine in both humans and Gods. In many religious traditions God is seen as masculine. But Makarand is here underscoring the Indian understanding of *Ardhanarisvara*, where the divine is half female and half male.

It is this union of male and female, this interplay between the author and his partner, this love between God and Goddess, this complementarity between *linga* and *yoni*, between yin and yang...this is the true source of fulfilment and joy...and much pain.

The fiery intensity of the images and writing is such that this book can only be savoured slowly, with many pauses. In the end *Identity's Last Secret* is not a book about Makarand and Gayatri, but about each of us, our loyalties and betrayals, and our often futile, occasionally fruitful, efforts to find the kind of love that gives meaning to our lives.

—Siddhartha, environmentalist, cultural critic, interfaith peace activist, and founder of Pipal Tree and Fireflies Ashram, Bangalore

Identity's Last Secret offers its confluent wisdom to every reader. As we traverse varied windows of consciousness in time and circumstance, we will find our deepest impulses reflected in the layered unfolding of this book.

—Vandana Kohli, author and filmmaker

"A great deal of poetic work has arisen from various despairs," wrote Lou Andreas-Salomé, the first woman psychoanalyst. Albert Camus said that "there is no love of life without despair of life." As an artist, I have come to understand despair as a divine experience. Makarand R. Paranjape's *Identity's Last Secret* is a true example of this divine human experience expressed with creative vitality.

Makarand says this book is "about a difficult relationship and its aftermath." What is this relationship? With whom? If you dive deep into his world, it's a relationship between naked truths that are never comforted. This "divine discontent", this "divine injustice", this state of inner tension is the source of his artistic energy, sometimes manifested as eroticism, sometimes as spiritual awakening. It's the oneness that every heart seeks.

—Vivek Ranjan Agnihotri, filmmaker and author

IDENTITY'S LAST SECRET

Makarand R. Paranjape

Blu print
An Imprint of
BluOne Ink

Title: Identity's Last Secret
Author: Makarand R. Paranjape

ISBN: 978-81-949547-9-8
Edition: I

Published by:
BluOne India LLP

Publisher's Address:
306, Tower-I, Assotech Business Cresterra,
Plot No. 22, Sector 135, Noida.

Website: www.bluone.ink
Email: publisher@bluone.ink

Printed in India at Thomson Press (India) Ltd.

Blu print

An Imprint of
BluOne Ink

For

Gayatri,
my wife—
this third lease of life

Foreword

All great art makes us see. Afresh, anew. Beyond the constrictive horizons of our usual view. It makes us feel and become a radically different way of looking. And it embeds this *anubhava* in our DNA.

For once we encounter such art, something fundamental immediately changes in us. Something beyond the mind, in the depths of our marrow, through the tympanum and the diaphragm, opens the third eye. The blinds and veils over our *drishti* fall off and an utterly radical sense and knowing is realised.

In the ancient Indic tradition, the *kavi* was not just a versifier. He could see farther than our limited shores, and he could reveal. And his word was the creative Word which could build Universes. The *kavi* gave his entire life in the pursuit of bringing forth the revelatory word.

Such was the bold and profound aspiration with which the Indian civilisation began its journey thousands of years ago. That it could create a macrocosm called Bharata from these insights, in art as in literature, in sculpture as in music, in economics as in polity, in warfare as in spirituality, is testimony to the power of its vision.

Identity's Last Secret is Makarand R. Paranjape's most audacious work in mixed media bringing together many of his avatars in one—as poet, philosopher, critic, scholar, interpreter—along with a 'graphic' art that builds upon his lifetime of creative adventures. It is a visual poem in the tradition of concrete poetry by George Herbert and Dylan Thomas. It alludes deftly to the Japanese art of Sumi-E with its intermedia play of simple and elegant brushwork alongside renka or haibun. But for the first time that I am aware, it recreates the ancient art of tantric scrolls that juxtapose meditative art with *beeja* mantras or invocations. Mandalas and yantras depict the inwardised space of a yogi's consciousness and the rhythms of accompanying verse bring a synesthesia of sound and vision.

In the final stages, the poet himself becomes the highest yantra or instrument in whom the divine is firmly established. As he becomes the *adhara* for a higher consciousness, his own base movements and nature transmuted in tantric alchemy, his heart, mind, and body become the layers that unveil one by one the deity within.

In the tradition of James Joyce and T.S. Eliot, Makarand has created a new form to represent the geometric configurations of the spiritual journey. But more than the technique, it is the clarity of description at each milestone that turns his art into meditation. The intense and raw feelings of loss, loneliness, betrayal, anger, avarice, and sexuality metamorphose into a resonant silence and peace. Makarand has chronicled the inner life of a *sadhak* under the guidance of his guru in a unique experiential manner, disrupting the usual genres of literature similar to the *Ulysses* or the *Wasteland*.

Makarand's journey is a synthesis of the inner and the outer, with a slow and developing insight of who he really is. Neither body, nor mind, nor feeling. Neither intelligence, nor ego, nor even knowledge. But something entirely and fundamentally different that is at once transcendental and immanent, individual, and universal. And he deconstructs himself following the map of his intensely human and lived explorations.

He does not reject any aspect of existence. He accepts the physical as well as the mental, the philosophic as well as the psychological, the romantic as well as the spiritual. But in his total acceptance, paradoxically, he is liberated from each knot in his awareness. In his embrace of the earth, the yogi grows de-identified and wide as the sky. Realising the truth of his final unity with all, he becomes blissful, fulfilled, settled, free.

In the Indic tradition, tantra is the transformation of the human into the divine. What most philosophies and religions avoid, abhor, and abnegate, tantra seizes upon as a means and a medium. It accepts the fierce, the terrible, the hideous and the lowly as valid modes of ascent. It rejoices in God as Rudra just as it venerates God as Vishnu. For God is not only Mahalakshmi but also Mahakali. And God is not only in temples and meditation halls but also in cremation grounds and battlefields.

I cannot remember last when an established writer of Makarand's stature took such risk and upended established literary conventions. Perhaps a D.H. Lawrence would have appreciated, for didn't he say that great literature changes one's blood-consciousness?

Perhaps a Kamala Das with her extremely frank and straightforward poems and autobiography which scandalised a generation of respectable critics and readers would have understood. Or a Pritish Nandy who sang of *Calcutta* in his youth as his beloved and tormentor.

To paraphrase the Torah, great art is not your uncle. It is an earthquake. It does not offer excuses or alibis, justifications, or apology. It shows honesty, frankly. It takes that which titillates or stimulates and makes it an object of contemplation.

Makarand attempted a similar visual poem in the *Confluence*, his exploration of Vedanta. Here, he has freed up the visual element even more intensely. For which literary figure of repute would dare place a Courbet nude along his highly chiseled verse. Only someone who has enough confidence in his power to match the highly sensational and controversial image and turn it into a symbol and an object of dhyana.

To my mind, Makarand is one of the finest literary and cultural critics and scholars of modern India. However, his refinement is not limited to intellectualism only. In the highest tradition of Indian poets and writers, he is also a seeker of truth. A truth that is inclusive and fearless. That is integral, noble, and grand.

Makarand's journey pursues the same seismic shifts as great art and revolutionary philosophic and psychologic insights. And with each successive work he becomes more tectonic and more implosive. *Identity's Last Secret* is his next earthquake in our comfortable and complacent living rooms. From him, we would have it no other way.

– Pariksith Singh, MD

Contents

Guru

Yogi Ramsuratkumar, Tiruvannamalai:
"If you want God alone, why do you accept the existence of anything else?"

Invocation

Dispeller of darkness within,
bolt of sheer lightening,
I seek refuge in your radiant being:
Ayeem, Ayeem.

Beholding such splendour,
irresistible adventure,
at last I cease to falter:
Hreem, Hreem.

Alphabet of bliss,
beginning of all being,
I yearn only for thy kiss:
Kleem, Kleem.

Puissant, immense, resplendent,
ablaze in darkness transcendent,
I delight in your secret name:
Shreem, Shreem.

1

Mantra

It is only when the mantra manifests
as a real person
can the seeker's sadhana or self-making be perfected.

When found,
such a fortunate spouse, paramour or partner
becomes the means,

apparatus and instrument of ascendence.
A veritable living incantation,
the mantra reveals

the true purpose of life.
In unfolding cosmic harmony,
it bridges the human and the divine.

For Hindus, the Gayatri is considered one of the most powerful of mantras.

Occurring in the Rig Veda (Mandala 3.62.10), it invokes Savitṛ, the solar deity, who represents higher consciousness.

Attributed to Rishi Vishvamitra, Gayatri refers to the metre in which the mantra is composed. Three eight-syllabled lines, or "a triplet of three divisions of eight syllables each" (*Monier-Williams*) make up twenty-four units, each to be clearly pronounced and uttered.

A mantra to practically any deity, even one's own guru, may be composed in this metre to render it potent and efficient.

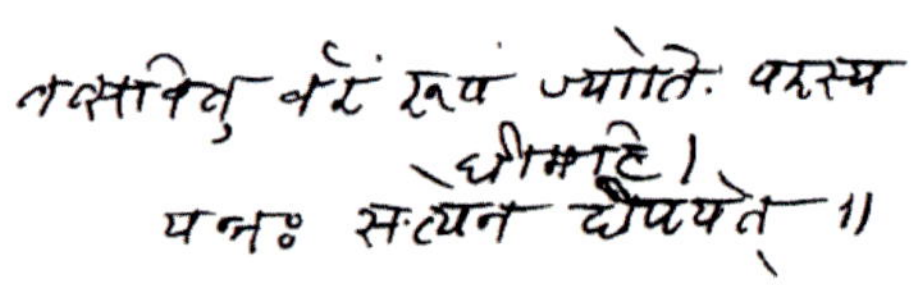
तत्सवितुर्वरं रूपं ज्योतिः परस्य धीमहि। यन्नः सत्येन दीपयेत्॥

Tat savitur varam rupam jyotih parasya dhimahi,
yannah satyena dipayet

Sri Aurobindo's Gayatri Mantra, in his own handwriting

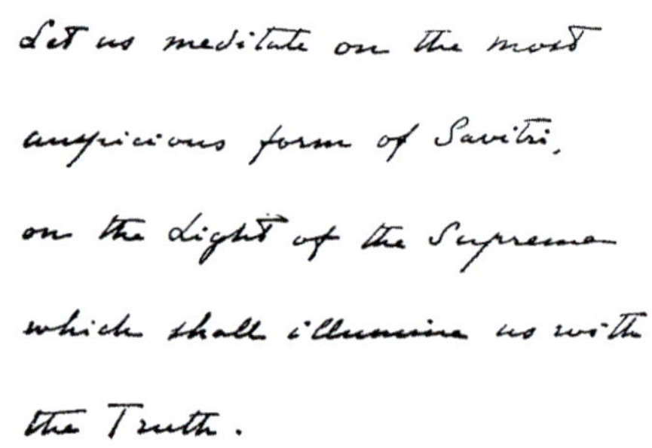
Let us meditate on the most
auspicious form of Savitri,
on the Light of the Supreme
which shall illumine us with
the Truth.

Rendered into English in the handwriting of his spiritual partner, Mirra Alfassa, better known as the Mother

According to the Yaska, the word *gayatri* is derived from *gai,* "to praise," plus *tri* (three), thus, to praise thrice. Or from *gam* (to go) plus *tri* (*gamtri* becoming *gayatri* through metathesis) meaning, to go thrice. Gayatri, the thrice-going mantra. Or, as Lakshman Sarup puts it, the "three coursed" mantra.[1]

In the Shaivaite traditions, Gayatri is the consort of Parashiva, the supreme, blissful, eternal, absolute, manifesting in the sun as Shivasurya. He is also Bharga or Sadashiva, whose consort, Manonmani, is the mantric form of Gayatri.

1 *The Nighaṇṭu and the Nirukta*, tr. by Lakshman Sarup, 2nd ed. (Delhi: Motilal Banarsidass, 1969): "Gayatri is derived from (the root) *gai,* meaning to praise, or from *gam* with *tri* by metathesis, i.e. three-coursed" (p. 119). See also James and Margaret Stutley, *A Dictionary of Hinduism: Its Mythology, Folklore and Development, 1500 B.C.–A.D. 1500* (1977; rpt. London: Routledge, 2019), p. 97.

Images of the pauranic Gayatri begin to appear around 10th century CE. She is often shown with five heads and ten arms. This famous painting of Goddess Gayatri is by Raja Ravi Varma.

Sometimes, Gayatri is identified with Kamadhenu, also known as Surabhi. She is the wish-fulfilling Goddess-Mother, the cow of plenty, who contains within her all gods and goddesses.

The *Taittiriya Aranyaka* (2.11.1-8) explains how the mantra should be chanted. First "Om," (ॐ) should be intoned, then the three great utterances, *mahāvyāhṛtis*, or mystic words, bhūr bhuvaḥ svaḥ (ॐ भूरभुवः स्वः), followed by the actual mantra.

ॐ भूर्भुवः स्वः
तत्सवितुर्वरेण्यं
भर्गो देवस्य धीमहि।
धियो यो नः प्रचोदयात्।

oṃ bhūr bhuvaḥ suvaḥ
tatsaviturvareṇyaṃ
bhargo devasyadhīmahi
dhiyo yo naḥ prachodayāt

From the world of *bhu*,
there is return, rebirth.

In *bhuva*,
thought and form still persist, albeit subtly.

But from *sva*, realm of spirit,

there is no more suffering, bondage, embodiment.

Sri Aurobindo translates it thus: "We choose the Supreme Light of the divine Sun; we aspire that it may impel our minds."[2]

The verb *prachodayāt* suggests vigorous exciting, instigating, driving, propelling, bestirring, inflaming, impelling.

The deity is thus invoked, in trans-procreative metaphors, to induce, force, propel, grasp, push forward by dint of the intellect the higher reality of supreme consciousness.

[2] *Evening Talks with Sri Aurobindo*, 4th rev. ed. (Pondicherry: Sri Aurobindo Ashram, 2011): pp. 58–59.

Verso

Edvard Munch, “Love and Pain,” Munch Museet, Oslo, Norway

Every relationship is potent and charged. It is, veritably, a power and energy exchange. This is our daily experience, if we are even a little self-aware.

When the exchange is also erotic, the energies are intensified, whether for better or worse.

But few realise that this is also true of every work of art.

Edvard Munch's "Love and Pain" is an attempt to clasp this idea in a tight embrace.

In this fin de siècle painting, the man, utterly submissive, is apparently comforted by a woman with flaming hair.

Her orange and red tresses stream over his bowed heard, engulfing him. On closer observation, they seem to cut across his face and her own arms like bloody gashes.

Was its hint of sado-masochism shocking to its early viewers? The painting was considered scandalous when first unveiled.

Some interpreted the woman's lips fastened on his neck as more than a mere kiss. Hence, it was also called "Vampire," though not by the artist himself.

Years later, the Nazis would pronounce it "morally degenerate."

The subject, evidently, fascinated Munch. He painted six different versions of it between 1893 and 1895.

Munch, of course, is best known for "The Scream," a painting that depicts horrors, arguably pertaining to modernity, too unspeakable to voice in words. The terrors and alarms of a nuclear holocaust, even?

Love can be catastrophic.

Or love and catastrophe go hand in hand.

Desire destroys not just individuals, but entire families, neighbourhoods, cities.

But can we resist it?

The desire, the fatal attraction of destruction?

In Alain Resnais's *Hiroshima Mon Amour* (1959), the screenplay was written by Marguerite Duras (New York: Grove Press, 1961). It contains one of the most significant expressions of doomed desire.

Paradoxically, the exchange occurs when we don't even see them on screen—the French actress and the Japanese architect, who are the nameless lovers in the movie.

Instead, only dream-like images of a city fleet across the screen and our mindscape.

A city, perfectly functional and adequate if not grand and glorious, before it is utterly wrecked and devastated.

By the atom bomb.

Reni Celeste, writing in *Film-Philosophy,* describes the scene in "Love and Catastrophe: Filming the Sublime in Hiroshima Mon Amour":

> "The dialogue dissolves into a monologue of desire by the French actress accompanied by a monotonous hypnotic tracking shot where the camera flows steadily down the city streets, across bridges, along train tracks. Her utterances and the visual movement resemble the moments of deep passion moving toward sexual climax, but we see no lovers, just streets, onlookers, details, bicyclists, things being passed as if seen from handlebars of a bicycle" (www.euppublishing.com/doi/full/10.3366/film.2005.0038).

Just ordinary life, passing by, just a city fated to be destroyed.

"Streets, onlookers, details, bicyclists...."

No lovers.

The unnamed French actress, played by Emmanuelle Riva, intones the staccato lines in an incantatory monotone:

I meet you.

I remember you.

Who are you?

You're so good for me.

How could I have known that this city was made to the size of love?

How could I have known that you were made to the size of my body?

You're great. How wonderful. You're great.

How slow all of a sudden.

And how sweet.

More than you can know.

You destroy me.

You're so good for me.

Plenty of time.

Please.

Take me. Deform me, make me ugly.

Why not you?

Why not you in this city and in this night so like the others you can't tell the difference? Please...(24–25).

Wasteful Expenditure of Spendthrift Hearts

I

He resisted her forty months—her body offering—
slim-waisted, ample-breasted...but why objectify her,
or deliver a *nakha-shikha*, toe to top account of her allure?
Just this: she was desirable—from the very beginning.

Yet three years on, she still didn't inspire trust.
Was it too good to be true, this romance she tendered
—or not good at all? Bad, too bad, from the start:
rash, unreal, extreme, if not star-crossed?

Her final fling,
so badass and feckless, just before marrying the proverbial
suitable boy? Or his own sputtering, underconfident drive,
dribbling at last before curtains call?

He remembered
Kundera's "great secret of life" that "women don't look
for handsome men." (Would *age-appropriate* be
more apt in his case?) "Women look for men
who have had beautiful women."[3] If so, he qualified.
They had, all of them, been so. Alone again, was he now
past his own past? She set his flickering libido ablaze.
That was both her triumph and turn on. Vanquished,

he wondered, what was her design? By gifting herself,
had she seized control, with distracted, even determined
disregard for rules? But who sets the rules when it comes
to desire? Standard operating procedures of the desperate?

Ulterior motives disguised as mystery, more dangerous,
half-surmised, half-detected, it stalked him night and day,
lurking in the shadows. The riddle she was made him rear
and buck with dread. So dire that he pushed back. Almost

it ended there. Before they'd
only just begun. Except for those
words—had she not uttered
them, what would've happened?

[3] *The Book of Laugher and Forgetting* (New York: Alfred A. Knopf, 1980), p. 16.

Rather unexpectedly, across
his formidable desk, meant
as much to maintain distance,
as evoke doubtful splendour—

beyond his remotest probabilities,
her words were not just terms
of endearment but a pronouncement.
Despite his negative salesmanship,

the rehearsal of failures, litany of lacks,
botched liaisons—serial deficiencies,
self-confessed, habitual heart breaks?
And his age, *fifty*, well almost, and she

not yet twenty-five. Half his age also
meant double the trouble, improbability,
non-workability in a relationship, let alone
durability. What lay ahead? Abandonment,

heartbreak, death of hope, lost kingdoms
shattered worlds, wrack and ruin, dregs
of discarded years, wreck on wreck,
stockpiles of loss. No precious metal but

mere dross, mounds of ash, wasted lives.
His story, so sad and sorry in its multiple
misfortunes, which interested *no one...*!
Carried away in the telling, he paused.

She listened impassively, head bowed, gaze down.
Then raising her eyes straight at him, she silenced
his recitation with a quiet, decisive, nod.
An assertion so sudden and surprising,

just like that, out of nowhere,
to his wide-eyed alarm, she said,
"I can give you a life." So taken
aback, he stared at her, speechless.

What the fuck!—his inner voice, overtaken by surprise,
reacted: over-confidence or scam? Was he so messy—
and easy? Or she so cocky, conceited, wishing to buy
him with counterfeit flattery or just the swag of youth?

Was giving someone a life so simple? *No, I don't think so*!—
That is not how it happens.
That is what he wanted to say,
but couldn't utter a word.

II

But how wrong I was. You crossed not just the massive
defence of my desk, that barricade separating my private,
self from the public, but also every pedantic blockade.

That very afternoon
you sought refuge,
bent over, wrecked

with sobs, a slip of a girl with eyes that hungered to swallow
the moon, now beset with huge, racking moans, sputtering
unshed tears, too dry to cry, shaking with choked gasps.

A breakup,
another,
yet another, fissure,

which even you couldn't escape with nubile, adolescent flippancy.
You grieved intensely with the clotted agony of growing up
too soon, before your time: "Very early in my life it was too late."[4]

The traumas of womanhood you negotiated with outright lies
and half-truths. Another devastation, in a long line of inevitable
breakups. My turn to shoulder the burden in a spasm of silence.

Your tale was dreadful: since not yet fourteen, you had taken to love
as to a project, a career almost. Ill-fated from the start, a quest
so private, so compulsive, an ageless need sprung from so deep

that it resembled some birth defect or childhood deformity.
You created love out of thin air, conjuring it from
the merest will-o'-the-wisp, making up lovers from

well-nigh nothing, making out with them, banking on them,
investing in one after another, even the worthless and unlikely,
in repetitive series, *sorties*—doctors, sailors, pilots, salesmen,

profligates, photographers, pensioners, prisoners,
crooners, cricketers, bankers, interns, white boys,
black dudes, bachelors, bigamists, bigots...[5] Giving

yourself to each, too soon exposing the ancient gash,
an unhealing wound, till the bubble burst as it would. Then,
the gnashing of teeth, weeping, *sweeping*, desolation. Alone.

Till the next sympathetic support became available. Mine?
I wondered too late with the horror of the doomed. Clouded
by abasement and infirmity, I couldn't see it clearly then.

4 Marguerite Duras, *The Lover* (New York: Pantheon Books, 2011), p. 4.
5 Duras clinches it in *Practicalities*: "You have to be very fond of men. Very, very fond. You have to be very fond of them to love them. Otherwise they're simply unbearable" (New York: Grove Press, 1993), p. 41.

How singular you seemed, how alone in your appalling loss,
as the forsaken and deserted in love are. Seeing you stagger in,
doubled over in pain, no thought or hesitation crossed my mind.

Instantly, instinctively, I reached out, crossing the self-imposed,
inviolable barrier. A fatal fall? With that single gesture I felt
compromised. The touch was light, even inconsequential,

but when you looked up in startled gratitude, momentarily
interrupting those shallow, shattering sobs, did I espy a succinct
second of triumph? Had you drawn me out, played me—and won?

I consoled himself, as if setting
the limits of my involvement:
"I'll see you through this; that's it."

A misadventure inadvertently undertaken, now so clearly stated,
did I think I was safe?
In retrospect, I feared I was already lost.

III

Having defeated him, would she let him off
the hook? How naïve to think so. Had she crossed

his mammoth hump of resistance for naught?
Wasn't hers a well-planned and practised assault?

The initial breach admitted, all the rest followed, as matter
of course. The swift, primal force of Eros or just sex?

To salve his conscience, he managed to postpone
the coup de grâce till she was out of his professional

orbit. But just about; she scoffed at his scruples, hardly
brooked delay. Despite the allure it held, he never

crossed that Rubicon of desire. He felt tripped, false-footed,
stripped of his resolve, reserve, and dignity. Dangled,

diddled. Then it was upon him, the time of transgression.
There was no turning back. "The *virtue* of restraint vs.

the *sins* of the flesh—tell that to the dead, six feet under—
or those who feel no pleasure." She laughed, full-throated,

with undisguised derision and delight. He looked at her
wonderingly: so young yet so carnal? Now she became teacher.

Once the barrier, border, tissue, sheath, carapace of constraint,
was breached, unrestricted caress ensued. There was no pretence,

no holding back. *Karezza* gave way to full-throated,
honey-dipped sensuality. Lawrence's blood religion,

taken to the meridian, cresting repeatedly, breaking,
resurfacing, a secret diurnal ritual, wonderous. Nightly

desecrations, torments unbearable, eventide flare-ups,
out of orbit, excursions, endless suspense, *sublimity*.

Abhisarika, Guler c. 1750's (V&A)

IV

Like an *Abhisarika*[6] she came, hesitant at first, tremulous,
breathless at the threshold. Then swiftly crossing, sure stepped,
with eager ingress. Her welcome, a homecoming, no longer some

dirty secret or injury. But how famished she appeared, eating
nothing all day, like a fasting pilgrim. First feasting at his table,
then indulged in bed, she brought herself to gasping ravishment.

Again their nightly rite of recurrent passion: bodies dappled in
tawny dew, exerted till they gleamed in the dark, ablaze.
He, a shining deity, and she, the naked naiad of the waters.

Thrashing about, a wayward nymph, glimmering with allure,
she deliberately and repeatedly damaged him. Prone and supine,
underneath he lay, as if blinded, immobilised, incapacitated.

Sensations so intense they brooked no resistance or interruption,
such leniencies and liberties tendered, ecstasies exceeding ardour
pleasure overcoming languor, irresistibly recovering desire.

Glistening and sodden, brimming from atop, she careened
into quiet, almost private convulsions. Rapture so fine
that he could barely feel her elation. In secret reverie,

she quivered to marvellous arousal. As to a sacred spring
she led his index finger into the misty
helix—then a sudden, swift, abrupt

reversal, as she flipped over. How she clung to him,
clutching him from beneath, an aching, grasping emptiness
drawing him even deeper, with an arching, throbbing craving,

awaiting the finish. Perched above, swooping low,
relentless in hunt, looming, decisive, secure and sure,
he pinned her low for the final assault that tolerated

no rebuff. At last, after a shuddering shock, she caved,
collapsing in disarray. Clothes, bed linen scattered, rudely
dispensed with, plucked off—dishabille in rout.[7]

[6] Literally, the one who ventures. According to the classical classification, going back to Bharata's *Natyasastra* and right through to Keshavadasa's *Rasikapriya* (16th century), there are eight types of heroines, or Ashtanayika. They recur throughout Indian music, dance, sculpture, painting, and literature. See Harsha Dehejia's *Rasikapriya: Ritikavya of Keshavdas in Ateliers of Love* (New Delhi: DK Printworld, 2013) for a practitioner's exposition. There are further classificatory divisions based on age, birth, rank, qualities, body types, and personality traits.

[7] "Liberation is achieved through enjoyment. Happiness is gained through enjoyment. Therefore, by every effort, a Sadhaka should become an enjoyer." —*The Yoni Tantra,* vol. 2., trans. Michael Magee (Harrow: World Tantra Project, 1995), p. 21.

The last shreds of pretence rented, ancient burdens, guilty
secrets disclosed, disowned, her fever broke in screaming
silence. Emptiness was banished, separation repealed.[8]

Despair dispelled, the roseate flowering of her eyes
brought to her lips a smile delicate, distinct, refined. Like
rare perfume, it spilled across benighted paths.

The metropolis shrouded in the slumbering fog, benumbed,
except for twin-burning, incandescent flames, was lost
to itself. In the early morning daze, the city keeled over, snoring

in porcine and insensate gloom. Across the darkened margin,
dew-struck, wrapped in the musk of a splendorous lust,
she departed, as if scattering gold dust on her way.

Night after rhapsodic night she returned
a svelte sylph, gliding iridescent in moonlight,
magnificently supped, sated, then requited.

[8] "Women are divine, women are life, women are truly jewels. Always have intercourse with a woman and meditate, whether she be one's own woman or not."—*The Yoni Tantra,* vol. 2, trans. Michael Magee (Harrow: Worldwide Tantra Project, 1995), p. 24.

V

He watched her gliding form, waving once, then receding.
Soon she vanished sprite-like, glowing elysian swirl,

steadily swallowed by the inky cloak of night.
He felt at first a gush of relief, like wind escaping a balloon

at bursting point—she was gone! Elation almost.
He could return to himself, nothing broken, seared,

as yet. Safe,
still alive.

But, immediately, a stab of pain,
a blade turning, twisting—

this having and losing her
night after night,

this returning to an empty bed...
Ah! such desolation of the spirit:

he was taken by a dread
he dared not name.

It was not merely from missing her till he was sore. Worse,
far grimmer, he was afraid, worried, harassed, appalled.

What if she never came back? Worse, what if she *did*?
Deck afire, hull blasted, his ship-self was out of kilter.

She drove him not only to distraction, but destruction:
what if she did something strange or crazy? Or foolish

or grossly imprudent, abominable? What if she hurt herself
or damaged him? What would happen if.... At the least

gossip, scandal, ruined reputation; then vengeance, retribution
swift, merciless, sharp as a curved scimitar, slicing right

through his standing, leaving him tattered. An anxiety
he could not name seized him. His fright was appallingly real.

Horror beyond surmise or grasp, phantom shapeless and obscure,
it left him paralysed, panic-stricken. He was misplaced;

bewitched, lost, he had turned into something else. Stranger
to himself, missing person, creature of nocturnal haunts,

werewolf,
vampire.

And yet nothing happened. Nothing
at all. She returned every evening

dodging time and tide for their breathless, dusky tryst.
Over and over again. Some days so tired was she that

immediately she curled up after dinner, asleep in his
arms. Waking up after midnight, with the other hunger

how she clasped him then, wide-eyed, recumbent,
or prone, pulling him down now, then pushing

him out. With each gasp, peaking
yet again, until she tipped over—flat

on her chest, her back and gleaming derrière, bare.
Looking at him unashamed, she took him back in

till he was done for, gone.
Lifeless, so useless now.

But she did not release him.
Fastening on him, she brought

him up once more, drawing him
out, like an unsheathed sword

fervently, ferociously. He heaved, whole being a-tremor.
Shaking with a shock so unbearable, he collapsed, wasted.

Falling into a torpor, he lay immobilised. His soul
extracted, like one of the living dead, pierced, destroyed.

Impaled, depleted, incapacitated, he forgot all about her
or the world. Motionless in bed, staring at the ceiling,

he heard the air conditioner's hum, while she quickly dressed,
gathered her things. He heard the front door shut, the latch

sound at the wicket gate, then fading footsteps. Deathly silence
seized his stricken soul as he passed into the land of the lifeless.

VI

Still, those were the happiest times. Nothing was certain,
yet everything possible. There were no promises made
or broken, no pledges, no betrayals. Life was liquid.
Pure elation. Even the fights weren't mad or merciless.

After all, we had only those four or five hours,
with their daily aptitude, *amplitude,* for discoveries,
triumphs. Copulation but also conversation, poetry,
music. Swapping childhoods, family yarns, sharing

emotional or sensual histories. Ghosts of previous lovers,
old traumas and scars, myths and legends, codes to live by,
wounds and vulnerabilities, scraps and shards of being,
passions to trade and hide—so much to do, so little time.

But together at eventide, night after brimming night.
That steadied us, gave us ballast. No estrangement, nor
treachery. Occasionally, when I was away, absent from
her arms, you cried of solitary afternoons or nights.

Then a great terror seized you, you confessed: "I'm afraid
you'll never come back. I feel unsure, apprehensive
of the future." What did it hold in store for you, for us?
So to the inevitable popping of the "L" word, so long unsaid,

withheld, postponed, and feared. The crucial, critical question
neither dared to raise though it loomed large, like a bird of prey
hovering over our innocent, anxious heads. Was it *love,* really?
Full of doubt, we could think of nothing else. Carelessly,

you retorted "I couldn't care." But in bed, the truth came
out. What happened each night was not lies. It could not be
refuted or overlooked. Like a devotee, I ministered to you
till your very pores sang hosannas. Each night, you rejoiced,

while my body, sweated with exertion, shone with godly sheen.
Whatever tricks our minds played, our bodies couldn't cheat
or deny us. Yet why didn't we make plans or own up to
the immensity of our clinch? Did we know more, perhaps,

with the unerring instinct of the deceived, than we dared to admit?
That upon the admission of such impossible love a cruel fate
awaited us? To acknowledge it was only to hasten the end.
I was haunted, alarmed, both by the enormity and ruthlessness

of truth. This realisation, and my own commitment,
I tested in myriad unsparing ways,
until I knew the fault line or fatal flaw
would not be denied or dismissed.

VII

She led the way here as well. Starting out, she'd declared,
"Getting you for free, I don't have to pay out of pocket
to try you out." Startled, slightly offended by her blunt
directness, I still admired her for the admission. No need

to varnish or whitewash our reality. Emotions, too, after all,
were just facts, though another species of experience.
"Right now, it costs me nothing to love you. But tomorrow,
who knows? I wouldn't like to barter vulnerabilities with you.

Our bond must mean more." I marvelled at her *bon mots*.
She seemed so full of relationship nostrums. Later, however,
those very metaphors of hoarding and splurging would pinch her.
But agony-aunt like, she continued to preach what she couldn't

practice. She failed at each of her own lessons or teachings.
Instead, she broke down. Waif turned monster. Her possessive
rages could only be called manic. She was jealous—of anyone,
anything that threatened to dislodge her from the sole centre

of my life—mother, daughter, ex-wife, former lover, friend, cook,
gardener—none must draw me away from her. All were enemies.
She had no sympathy for anyone; she had suffered too much
to care for others' miseries or woes. Let them rot in hell, she raged.

All my consideration, attention, must be reserved for her alone.
If I dared tend to another, it was always at her expense, hence
unforgivable. She would never let me forget it. Upbraiding me,
abusing the imagined competitor, she extracted attention, by fits

and tantrums. Love, when it came, turned out to be
baje khoroch, wasteful expenditure, reserved only
for spendthrift hearts. Those who can't keep their wealth
but squander it in shopping malls filled with lonely souls.

When I had wavered
before the fall, she
taunted me: "Disable
the goddamn firewall. You can't have relationships in safe mode!"

She proffered temptation after alluring temptation,
each transgression exciting, each danger thrilling,
each gratification enticing. But all these she wrapped
in just one word, *Love,* with its accompanying wisdom:

"What's life worth without *Love*?" she admonished me,
"and what's *Love* if not risky business?" When I conceded,
"Good," she cried, "but whatever happens, you must swear
to one thing. You must *Love* me alone, no one else."

That one caveat remained: she above all others,
she more than all the loves of my life—
before or after, she must be the top bitch.
On that there would be no compromise.

Without that, *nada*; no relationship, no sex,
no love, no friendship even, nothing.
In every assignation, every confrontation,
she was always the top, I the bottom.

Or so she pretended, regardless of consequences.
For her, full control, no holds barred; for me
no respite or retreat. Submission to the point
of shameful thraldom. She must rule or I would die.

VIII

So she checked my mail, read my journal by night—
no question of seeking permission. Compulsively looking
for that faintest trace of betrayal, she always found it,
an excuse to berate or punish me. Anything to tighten

her stranglehold, the noose that she held me by. She always
found what she was looking for. A prior partner or relationship
in another country before we became a couple. Though
I never lied to her, there were things I had kept to myself.[9]

For months after, she flayed me for past wrongs. Later,
desperate to settle scores, recklessly she cheated on me.
"Come on, be a man. Get over it!"—her response to my outrage.
Perhaps, she was right. No point crying over spilt milk.

But that didn't stop her from prying into my things, rifling
through my laptop, her *sauten*, co-wife, rival, as she named
it. She opened cupboards, drawers, bookshelves, and my safe.
There must be no dilution, no remission, of her power.

Every relationship decision became a struggle to maintain
her dominion, assert her power. Hadn't she earned that right,
learned her lessons from her mother? Only total capitulation
by the man could signal victory, only then could she lower

[9] "When sex is at stake, the truth just goes out the window"—Sara Scribner's review of Clancy Martin's book, *Love and Lies: An Essay on Truthfulness, Deceit, and the Growth and Care of Erotic Love* (New York: Farrar, Straus & Giroux, 2015), https://www.salon.com/2015/02/14/when_sex_is_at_stake_the_truth_just_goes_out_the_window_clancy_martin_on_love_lies_and_final_first_kisses/

her guard, suspend her threats or charms. Until then,
all-out war. If I still didn't understand, she spelled out
the terms: when it came to her, resistance was futile.
Only utter submission would bring cessation of hostilities.

To that end, she remembered and reiterated the smallest slight,
the slightest infringement or curtailment of her entitlement.
She meticulously toted up misdemeanours or infringements,
later to hold me to account, interest compounded with principal.

Exacting her dues, penalties added for lapses, any neglect
or inattentiveness to her demands only meant an extra charge.
"What is your main job?" she asked, supplying the answer herself
as I stood chastised, downcast, knowing some dire sentence

was about to be passed—"*Only* to attend to me, *only* comfort me.
I ask for *nothing* else, nothing more. Not to be fed, clothed,
or even sheltered, all of which I can well do on my own.
Just this—be my emotional handler *on demand*—this I ask."

Was I to be typecast as the handler of her vulnerabilities? I asked.
"What else are relationships for?" she countered. "If you can't
do even that, you are utterly useless." Where *was* I when she
needed me the most? When her flatmate slapped her or when

she was hospitalised with a gut clogged so severely her innards
had to be flushed? Or when she was moving house, *why* wasn't I
there to carry boxes and bags? Did it matter that I was in another
country? No, I should have rushed to her side, dropping everything,

even at short notice, to minister to her needs and demands.
Why wasn't I around? Why did she have to turn to strangers?
At last I realised, that she was not quite well. I loved her but she
terrified me. Cornered, I consoled himself: she was complicated,

she was contradictory, but so extraordinary—it would be okay.
I loved her, after all.
Love countenanced all,
making up for shortcomings and pitfalls. I would find a way to make

it work. Make the crooked
places straight;[10]
somehow we would come into grace,
and be saved.

[10] Isaiah 45:2: "I will go before thee, and make the crooked places straight: I will break in pieces the gates of brass, and cut in sunder the bars of iron" (KJV).

IX

Gradually, he found himself translated.
She changed him completely, rendering him
unrecognisable not just to others, but to himself.
He became what he'd never imagined: in dress,
demeanour, bearing—even shaving his moustache
because it bruised her passionately kissing lips.

She invaded his life, seizing control. In one respect alone
he remained as he was. His secret, emotional self,
still precious, precarious, a diminutive deity protected
in a dark, inner sanctum. Distant, inaccessible,
jealously guarded by its high-priest intellect, it hid.
Embroidered curtains separated it from worshippers and lovers.

Including her.
Was it this she
could not forgive, this last self-protective barrier—
or was it something else
more sinister and ominous,
real, undeniable or invented, imagined?

Wherever they went—Delhi, Kolkata, Dakshineswar,
Tarakeswar, Pondicherry, Chennai, Bangalore,
Kasol, Manali, Srinagar, Agartala; or beyond—
Kuala Lumpur, Singapore, Ho Chi Minh City, Hui,
Bali, Ubud, Milan, Como, Bergamo, Venice, Rome, Norwich,
London—every single place—

she fought, bitterly, dramatically,
without shame or restraint,
raining tears, striking not with words alone,
but beating, biting, scratching, clawing, slapping.
She stormed out of hotels, trains, pubs,
bag and baggage, even in the middle of the night.

Such fits of rage, abuse, desperate outbreaks,
heaping unbearable insults,
in repeated bouts
of violence, invective,
taunts, tirades, attacks, tantrums.
in repetitive spells of fury.

She smashed things,
hurling whatever was handy
sometimes even aiming at him—
breaking phones,
cracking mirrors,
shattering computer screens.

In addition:
investigations,
interrogations,
inquisitions,
periodic censure and denigration,
recurrent litanies of his misdemeanours and her privations...

Bitter complaints
of how he had mistreated her
all these months.
So much drama, so much damage—
what was it for?
he wondered each time it ended.

Followed by
whimpering breakdowns,
abject apologetics,
sympathy-beseeching
justifications,
tearful make-ups,

relapsing into
infant-like supplications.
She would beg to be taken back,
readmitted to the confines and comforts
not just of home and hearth,
but of warmth and love.

An orphan or waif's
immense craving
for acceptance.
What did it all amount to?
What was the meaning of it,
this conundrum that was her?

X

Then her prison-break,
as she called it.
A break, from me, from *us*,
from the long-distance mortgaging of her youth,
her wonder-years
to her phantom Skype-lover,

the sheer pointlessness and absurdity of it!
Denied the solace of touch or tenderness
when it was most craved for,
plus all the thankless restrictions of fidelity—
"What for?" she cried,
"For an idea, ideal, or mere fantasy?"

She bit against the bridle,
and revolted.
On New Year's Eve she bid me goodbye,
weeping on the phone,
"I hope you don't think of me
as a promise-breaker..."

And added for good measure, "I truly loved you...."
With the fireworks and crackers going off
all about me in the smoky gloom,
I could hardly believe we could end like this,
four years literally going up in smoke,
just sound and fury signifying nothing.

So unreal because it was staged, spectacular,
unforgettable, unsurpassable—
this break if not break-up
that she'd engineered,
leaving me shell-shocked,
incredulous.

When I turned to her for some clarity,
closure,
she became pitiless:
"For your own good," she womansplained,
"I'm pushing you away. Don't try
to reach me."

It was scary,
not knowing where she was,
what she was up to,
who she was with.
I found it out later
as my worst nightmare coming true.

The horror that I had tried to avoid was now all mine.
Not just abandonment,
but the cuckolding,
never openly admitted,
but only to be guessed at.
Despite my stubborn clinging to the idea of her loyalty

it was revealed:
within ten days of the distancing,
she had moved in with another man,
paying, before long, the expected price.
The break-up, however, only proved
partial, for out of love or guilt

she started calling me again,
as if to resume,
but, no, the very next moment,
retracting, confirming
that my rights were
not yet fully restored.

As to her, *she* was free,
she reiterated,
to do as she pleased,
at least for the time-being.
"Oh, so are you leaving me?" I asked.
"Well...not yet, not *entirely*," she rejoined.

XI

Those days of longing and not having were the worst.
Insane jealousies, rages,
hatreds, old and new—
she had not only turned the tables on me,
but she had turned me into her.
Now I was a monster of jealousy and rage.

Though all signs were there,
my self-saving, self-serving delusions blinded me.
The tell-tale signs were obvious.
Her bold betrayals were
deliberately planned, indirectly disclosed,
but expertly executed.

She announced her second intended infidelity
quite insouciantly in her version of the nursery rhyme:
"The pussycat's going
to London to see the Queen,
scaring the little mouse there
under her chair."

Actually,
it was a broke girl's desperate lunge,
with borrowed money and plumage,
to find her long lost Continental lover,
earlier mismatched elsehow.
Now discovered to be a cancer survivor,
he didn't work out.
She then pronounced an end to our breakup,
inviting me to our last Tango, not in Paris,
but London.
She laughed and flirted,
"I'll be eminently fuckable[11]—like Maria Schneider!"

I remembered how gloomily and badly the film ends,
with Jeanne killing Paul,
after he chases her through the streets,
following her to her apartment.
When he tells her he loves her,
she reveals her name, then shoots him.

In London:
the street fight
right in the middle of Oxford Circus,
surrounded
by scurrying shoppers and commuters,
too polite to interfere.

Then the bizarre seduction in the pub
off Tottenham Court Road.
I bought her malts and bitters.
She drank and cried
disgorging and eviscerating
lumps of love, still mangy and dripping.

[11] For the pedantically pudic, the first usage has an Indian connection. It occurs in Capt. C. Devereaux's *Venus in India* (1889): "The poor man had at last outwitted his careful wife and obtained the much-longed-for fuckable cunt" (p. 110). According to *The F-Word* edited by Jesse Sheidlower (New York: Oxford University Press, 2009), "eminently fuckable," as a phrase, was used for the first time in James Jones posthumous novel *Whistle* (1978). Jones was the author of *From Here to Eternity* (1951), which became a famous, award-winning movie. He died at the age of 55. I have, however, found an earlier usage in *Meanjin Quarterly*, volume 29 (1970): "I said, you know, Julia dear, apart from anything else you are so eminently fuckable" (p. 456).

The loathsome finale,
back in my service apartment.
Fellatio. Then vomit.
The dread of those
desperate hours of lust and madness,
pining and rage, losing and finding,

played out in senseless, toxic cycles
of lust, lost, lust—
such a sure recipe for disaster and calamity.
The exact opposite and perversion
of the formula of successful love,
found, lost, found.

How I despised myself,
revolted at what she was doing to me,
hating her,
but despising myself worse.
Who*ever* behaved this way,
with herself or the one she loved!

I wanted to obliterate her presence,
or to die,
right there,
in that cold,
overcast, horribly cruel, world-capital,
babel of 150 tongues.

Perhaps only Othello was privy to that fatal urge,
the murderous rage
that she kindled in me.
Why?
Why was she doing this?
Why had she ruined me?

Was this the penalty of loving her?
Had I feared all this beforehand,
life's ambush and revenge
for tangling with a woman so non compos mentis:
the revenge of the Eros-eaters,
harrowing castration?

Was that why I had held out so long?
Knowing not by force of intellect
but sheer instinct of the condemned,
what she would do
upon my surrender,
the price she would exact for my fall?

Was this the bullet I wanted to dodge?
The searing trauma,
helpless haemorrhaging,
unstoppable pain,
unremitting grief,
from the deadly wound she would inevitably inflict?

Was I safe only as long
as I did not love her?
Once in love,
in her thrall,
she would show herself
for what she was,

la belle dame sans merci—
and I, "so haggard and so woe-begone"
the errant knight,
"starved lips in the gloam."
From verse to worse
raced my fevered mind.

Would I end up
hunted, *alone and palely loitering*?
Is this what I'd foreseen forty months ago,
with the prescience of the twice-distraught?
Had I wished to save myself from it,
mortally scared of what would befall if I caved or cared?

Is this what allowed me to cling on
to flimsy veils of precaution, disguised
as duty, family obligations,
above all, work?
I gave himself to writing, reading, lecturing,
ceaselessly venturing outward, throwing myself

repeatedly upon the non-existent mercies
of a mean and indifferent world, pouring
myself out till wasted, only to return home
drained, to a vacant bed. Cross-eyed,
hexed, exposed, and alone.
Is that what I had wished to avoid?

From the very start,
I could not fully trust who she was
or presented herself to be.
Was it because her favours were incredible?
Or because I discerned that she would
use them carelessly to dump and destroy me?

XII

And now it was done. He was wounded,
defaced, despoiled.

How could he
pull himself out of the pit he had fallen into of his own blunder?

What resources did he have to fall back upon? What remedies
prayers, charms, drugs, opiates?

It was when he was hurt so badly and felt
utterly lost, destroyed, shattered, broken in many parts,

that he stumbled upon the door
to her clandestine, subterraneous chamber of horrors.

Was this who she was,
what she did to those who made the fatal error of loving her?

Had he discovered it at last—her secret?
How she injured those who loved her and she loved?

She did not transfigure—
she *disfigured*

her lovers
before turning them out.

Now they were no good for anyone,
not even for her.

Was this it,
the ultimate humiliation,

obliteration, that he had tried to duck
but, finally,

insanely,
failed to dodge?

When the realisation dawned upon him,
he howled in pain and horror.

As had been ordained,
his suffering only increased with knowledge.

All his ju-jitsu proved useless. Her juju,
voodoo, proved so strong that it had to come from a source

primal and prehensile, defying analysis, healing, termination.
What could be such a woman's comeuppance?

He found himself deranged, damaged,
in the grip of payback psychosis:

no punishment was too mild for her, his unhinged mind screamed,
she should be crucified or tortured on the rack,

at last burned at the stake
like some medieval witch.

How did the universe permit such
perfidy, such extravagant perversion?

He laughed like a lunatic at his own prodigal furies:
surely, his sorrow had crazed him,

he who could not bear to imagine
the slightest injury to his oh so beautiful,

wild, *dhinglee*, whom he'd loved to distraction
so tenderly, desired so madly.

He wanted only to be returned
to the solace of her comforting breast.

But now he was ill, frenzied
in the contrary symmetry of craving and madness.

XIII

Did you fight so bitterly actually to save me from yourself?
Perhaps, you wanted to protect me from this violation
or stop yourself from being compelled wreak it on me,
like those accursed *femme fatales* of yore. I remembered
Medea, Clytemnestra, Delilah; or Helen of Troy, who destroyed
the entire ancient Aegean world. Wasn't Venus herself
the epitome of lecherous treachery, cuckolding the old,
ugly Vulcan, her crippled, blacksmith husband?
Perhaps you knew your deadly flaw.
Were your brawls meant only
to preserve me from you,
and from a fate worse than death?

Your fatal flaw, was a missing but vital part, like some congenital
curse. Irreversible damage caused by childhood abuse,
havoc meted out by a mother who was both progenitor and foe?
The feud carrying on in repetitive, unresolved, hurtful cycles,
births and deaths in hopeless recurrence, each wounding,
and in turn, wounded by the other, till you two,
mother and daughter, were locked together in an interminable
fatal embrace? Scarred continually with mutually inflicted stigmata,
wounds, ever-tender, never-healing, patches scarlet and purple
on hands, arms, shoulders, breasts, necks, bellies, and thighs,
throbbing with low intensity or flaring up agonisingly,
from time to time?[12]

Perhaps this primal damage or defect made it
impossible for you to settle down, the root of an instability
so basic and insurmountable, at the heart of your being.
It ensured you remained never fully formed,
never fully present to yourself or to your world.
Your element was chaos and night;
you sought out the storm like Lear on the heath.
There, exposed and unaccommodated,
you endured. Only in dire straits or emergencies,
only *in extremis*, could you bond or mate.
But in the end, you would break down—
to wound and be wounded again.

Even a big love or true lover could not heal you.
All they could do was contain your neurosis awhile.
You used men like meds, but could not keep a single man.
Before long you resumed acting out your practiced
privations—ecstatic unions, unbearable separations—
with repetitive but compulsive frequency,
complete with mock rings
and nervous breakdowns,
all the way to slashed wrists and hospitals.
Then, emptied out, you regressed,
a foundling, child-like and guiltless again,
waiting for another man, another escapade.

[12] "Our mothers always remain the strangest, craziest people we've ever met," Marguerite Duras, *Proclivities* (New York: Grove Press, 1993), p. 49.

From this crazy-making cycle, though myself disfigured
and damaged, I had to be freed. But was it already too late?
Was the die cast, the damning deed done?
Only remained the final blow, devastating and terminal.
When it did befall, it was not a bolt of lightning,
with storm and thunder. Almost a soft feather-touch,
no less lethal than the sharpest steel,
it cut so keenly that, at first, I felt no pain.
Then I knew I was bleeding to death.
Feeling light-headed as my senses slowly numbed.
I laughed out loud: "What the fuck, *I'm dying*—
and there's not even music...!"

XIV

What hope was there for him now?
Disarray within,
discord without?
Who could live with a woman so disorderly,
unruly and unstable? One whom he must constantly
be reacquainted with, as if encountering a new person
each time? Or worse, someone so familiar growing strange
over and over again?

What else could explain why she spelled out
at great length her grand, final declaration?
I want to be with you for the rest of my life, even afterwards.
I want to be yours as soon as possible, wherever that might be.
I'm willing to walk the line, walk down the aisle, if you'll have me.
Or just walk the road with you; I want to be with you till the end of days.
I'm ready to make a full and final commitment. You may not believe me,
and wonder if I'm saying all this from the deep fear of losing you.

I have given this profound thought, every minute I've been away
from you. But not because I cannot live without you, but because
that would be the single greatest mistake of my life. I've come to realise
that my heart was already given over to you—all of my blue lotuses
are yours. My very existence makes only partial sense without you.
So at last, I have this concrete offer: I want to be with you forever
from today until the end of days. Come back to me, my love,
right this instant. I cannot wait to be yours and make you mine.

So beautiful, so ruinous, this is what she had said.
just a month before her reckless infidelities.
Was it not something to hold on to and believe,
something to live by, if not plan a life?
But when he had returned,
only four weeks later,
he was met with another *fait accompli*:
"There is no 'us' anymore."

She said she had given up serving the cause of love;
it was thankless and futile.
She wanted peace now,
peace, which in response to her turbulence, he had proposed
at the very outset to be at the centre of their "big connect."
Big connect?
Her words for the love of her life,
the relationship of a lifetime with her soulmate.

Hadn't she exalted him as totally made for her,
filling both heart and womb, mind and body—
unto her very tomb?
Hadn't she anointed him as the chosen one,
offering all her heart's lotuses at the altar of his love?
Hadn't she proclaimed that their grand passion,
lasting longer than any of her past relationships,
would outlast her life?

Now he was back where he had begun,
alone, deserted, emptied, stark, anchorless, adrift,
no prospects, no past, no present, no future.
How had it all come to this?
The promise of great love, the love to end and surpass all loves,
a love that neither would outgrow nor outlive, how could it
end like this?
He was furious:
no one should be allowed to make such promises *ever*.

The universe itself should ban such avowals for their concealed deceit.
In their rotten heart is something that corrodes our faith
in the very order of things.
Truth of the moment?
No!
That simply would not do, could not
be excuse enough to make such grand, deceitful promises.
Oh the cheapness of momentary effect!

No instance of elation should be allowed
to engender decades of pain.
He was right to have doubted her;
her undertaking to spend a life with him,
had not lasted even a full month.
Of what value was such a person?
Yet why did he hurt, mourn, and pray so much—
phire esho—come back, for a person so worthless?

XV

When we'd just begun, she said she was not paying out
of pocket for her passions. Now she explained, as a matter
of fact, that her wallet was empty. Empty purse, *pussy*,
empty heart, too? Whom had she squandered it all on, then,
if it was really free? So much wasted expenditure?
And what of him? With no one to heed
to his need, he had no place to rest his head. Cast out,
in the raging wind, rain, and storm,
herself a pauper, she had bankrupted him too.
But why blame her, he thought inconsolably:
not she, but life itself had mistreated him thus,
giving unexpectedly, taking away as swiftly, without forewarning.
As if underscoring a lesson he did not wish to learn or having
learned it once or twice, possibly never wishing
to remember it or live by it.
What was this hardest
of lessons, a precept
he was resisting?
Was it to shed the foolhardy and naïve demand that life
be *fair*, people keep their *promises*, abide by their *word*,
deliver what they said they *would*? Why? Because *he* always had?
Therefore others also *should*? "Hon," she had said with a smile,
"you're an *original innocent*. Grow up."
But life taught him over again that the nature of things,
was not as he wished, or wanted, or ought to be.
That was not how Magna Mater ran her universe. Frequently,
had his fortunes met with abrupt, catastrophic reversals, especially
in matters of women. Apparently easy conquests turned too soon
into treacherous abandonments. Followed by a full-scale stripping
of privileges, being pushed out or purged from charmed circles.
Disinherited, cast out suddenly, callously.
Why was he disenfranchised so easily, so disgracefully?
How often had he been turned out,
unexpectedly, unceremoniously, *unjustly*!
Why?
What was the blight
that marked him apart from others,
that made him so easily recognisable
as *not* one of their own,
Therefore so easy to forsake?
Was it this very guilelessness that defined him?
Being so inept in the ways of the world,
let alone of (wo)men, was he to be
cut and slashed repeatedly for his truth-obsession,
the drive that no one
really cared for or valued, least of all the fairest of them?
Who would want to be shown up as changeable, vain, wicked?
Worship me, only me, was the vulvar demand. For it is only

I who succour and solace this side of eternity. As to the other side,
who has seen it or cares? Here, in the world of men, it is I who
rule and command obeisance. For that which dwells between
my shanks is the *origin of the world*.[13]

All deities and powers abide here.
Where do you think *you* came from, you little *prick*?
You, woman-born as the rest, must pay your dues
at the fountain of all virtue and profit, the one and only
sacred shrine of all mankind, elementary and original.
This is my domain, the world of men, given over to me,
to create, reign, and dispense favours. All bow to me,
fight over me, exalt me above everything, become my slaves.
Idiot, at least *pretend*, if you don't believe. You may treat us
as badly as you're likely to, once you coddle and flatter us to the hilt.
Sing hosannas to the high heavens, serenade us, fulfil
our every whim.
Then deal with us
as you must.
But to think that any woman will remain yours
if you value *truth* above her is to invite disaster.
Who *cares* for your truth? You may shove it up
where it best belongs, for it is nothing
but a load of shit. *Twat* is the highest truth.
Twat is all ye know on earth and all ye need
to know. To find happiness here, salvation
hereafter, adhere to this one formula; *twat* will
save you from so much distress and tribulation.[14]
T-t-t-twat.
The magic mantra divined,
he still remained mulishly obdurate, losing everything,
having wagered it all on some ramrod verity against which
every ship of sighs, hopes, longings, desires, fancies,
every romantic craft, was capsized or dashed to pieces.
So easy to love, so hard to abide,
is how she had once described him.
Still, after repeated
blows and bruisings,
no knowledge came to him.
The thing that he feared the most—the disowning
abandonment, dispossession, degradation, mortification,
—that cruel thing occurred again.

[13] L'Origine du Monde (1866) or "The Origin of the World" hangs in the Musee d'Orsay, on the left bank of the Seine in Paris. The painting of a woman's hair-covered vulva, painted from a low angle, with her face invisible, shocked Gustav Courbet's contemporaries and generations afterwards. Actually, till the museum acquired it in 1995, it was seldom seen, hidden behind a wooden door in the famous psychoanalyst-linguist Jacques Lacan's country home at Guitraneourt. Lacan's theory of the gaze is supposedly drawn from the painting:

> this is the essential point—the dependence of the visible on that which places us under the eye of the seer. But this is going too far, for that eye is only the metaphor of something that I would prefer to call the seer's 'shoot' (pousse)—something prior to his eye. What we have to circumscribe, by means of the path he indicates for us, is the pre-existence of a gaze—I see only from one point, but in my existence I am looked at from all sides.—*Four Fundamental Concepts in Psychoanalysis* (New York: W.W. Norton, 1978), p. 72.

Now it is reliably believed that Courbet did not callously portray just the woman's genitalia. A newly discovered fragment suggests that he also showed her face in an earlier version.
What Courbet possibly implied in this painting was widely regarded as true in India from ancient times: "Hari, Hara and Brahma, the gods of creation, maintenance and destruction—all originate in the yoni."—*The Yoni Tantra,* vol. 2, trans. Michael Magee (Harrow: Worldwide Tantra Project, 1995), p. 8.

[14] "The wise man should always avoid blame, disgust or shame of the yoni." —*The Yoni Tantra,* vol. 2, trans. Michael Magee (Harrow: Worldwide Tantra Project, 1995), p. 21.

XVI

But why? Why wasn't
he able to recognise it,
the figure in the mystery?

Then at long last it came
to him—the knowledge
that eluded understanding.

Since times immemorial,
birth after birth had he
searched for it in vain.

What was life's lesson
in the shape of woman—
mother, consort, daughter,

paramour teaching him?
Was it really so difficult to grasp, apprehend?
What he was so afraid of and tried so hard to evade—

that very thing, why did it pursue him,
extending the same teachings,
time after time?

Yes, he was rejected,
pushed out, expunged.
But never destroyed.

The damage was deep but
not fatal. Neither endless,
nor irreversible. Never

was he truly discarded,
unprotected till he bled
to a lonely, ignoble end.

On every single occasion, help came. Just when he thought he was
finished, a new beginning presented itself. If a door slammed shut
with a thud, a window creaked open unexpectedly. The message

life conveyed was exactly the opposite of what he had construed.
He had been protected, saved, not destroyed or discarded.
The lesson was not to despair, not to give up hope,

—but give up fear.
Not to be afraid ever.
The worst possible outcome

was not his,
nor anyone's
permanent portion.

The truth was
fear not, fear not, fearnot—
fearnotnot, fearfearnot,

fearnotnotnot, neverfearfear
everever, nevernever fear
fear not fear, not fear fear...

The message, recurring timelessly,
tirelessly,
as surmise and corroboration,

sunrise and sunset,
rain and shine
hill and dale,

oasis and desert,
land and sea,
pearl and oyster—

had somehow
thus far
been lost on him.

Put any which way,
it came down to the same thing.
Do not be afraid:

to live, to love,
to fail, to lose, to shatter
to die.

Pit to summit is what it is,
our daily grind,
until we get it right.

For the universe is not one-sided,
but compensatory,
both in her deprivations and excesses.

The whole, which is holy, is perfectly balanced,
squared, offset, ultimately settled—
not blemished, by deficits or surpluses.

XVII

The cosmic credo is unmistakable: *samatvam yoga uchyate*
—in equality,
equanimity—

is the stable union accomplished,
like the still centre
of the turning wheel.

Heartbreak is not a pleasant thing,
but it must not terrify us.
No fright must come between us and love.

For our nature is love:
we are not *in* love, nor *seeking* love,
we *are* love.

His original innocence was his greatest gift. It was his trustfulness that made him unafraid to love, no matter how crippling the heartbreak, how marring the scar, how disfiguring the ensuing bereavement.

To live is to love.
He would love to the very end,
to his dying breath.

He was not looking
for love—though love was good to find. His love
was no ruse, neither trick nor bargaining point.

Love's currency could not
be measured in terms of its buying power,
profit and loss.

It was
no *baje khoroch,*
wasteful expenditure,

of a spendthrift heart that could afford extravagance.
Love's very squandering,
added to its limitless store,

uncovered an endless trove of treasures,
augmented in sharing,
diminished in hoarding.

And how neatly his heart broke,
like a pod bursting its spores to the wind,
to be wafted where it list,

for another season of sowing.
What he so feared was only his destiny;
he could not escape it, try as he might.

For it had not been thrust
upon, but he had chosen it. Nothing could hold,
nothing bind or blind him.

He was free to be,
free to love.
Only in perfect freedom could love blossom.

Every heartbreak
was not so much a defacing
as preparing of the ground,
hoe turning up soil, rich and loamy, for a second seeding.
Love perfected conferred fullest freedom,
fearlessness abiding.

He was not exceptional but simple.
Love was simple too, the simplest
thingamajig there was.

Love was true: the only true thing really,
the what and the wherefore of the whole shebang,
the reason for everything.

Rather than denying it,
he had to learn, at last,
how to live

mottled, dappled
with love's stipple,
so easily recognisable.

For it was no mutilation at all,
no mark of Cain,
left by an angry deity upon a sinner's brow.

Nor the broken nose
of excommunication,
humiliation's stamp.

Not scarlet letter,
but red badge of courage, it was the kiss
of the rose of God.

The sign
that he was claimed,
and calmed.

More:
perhaps,
equipped with this special secret, he could finally find

what had eluded him so far—
lasting, not short-lived, felicity.
The company of the woman whom he loved,

but somehow
hadn't so far
been able to live down happily ever after.

Now, with true regard, he might
even kneel at the singular,
perennial fount of earthly joys,

without feeling pussy-whipped,
bushwhacked and broken
into submission.

His genuflection at the altar of all gratifications
might no longer
be insincere,

no act or pretence,
but earnest, acknowledged,
surrender,

true penitence,
accompanied by meaningful endeavour.
Could that really be possible?

He regarded himself
as in front of a looking glass:
he was gaunt,

furrowed,
but free.
There was still a vitality to him,

even jauntiness of step—
(*he moved so fast*).
How blithely he'd borne the burden of five decades.

There it was.
But so much still lay ahead,
by way of real accomplishment, realisation, recognition.

Being himself
seemed not so bad after all.
Thus living and giving—or just being alive.

XVIII

As far as he was concerned, one thing still remained
unclear, unsolved to him,
the puzzle of her love's enormous need,
what had made her wreck him.

Then,
suddenly, one day, he had an answer to that too:
the need of love such as this,
not so inconsiderable

as insensate, inconsiderate
—incredible—
demanded payment
in a special coin,

for it actually included and exceeded
all others.
Given its despotic demands,
such love needed a triple pledge,

as an ancient trinity band might seal,
eternal love,
fidelity unwavering,
joy everlasting.

Or something as grand,
if more Hindu: a union of all
three bodies, physical, subtle, and causal,
valid in all three worlds,

nether, terrestrial, and heavenly,
three times three.
Past, present, future. All three states,
waking, dream, deep sleep:

and beyond the three,
even unto the fourth,
never realised fully, except in its (im)possibility,
vaikhari, *madhyama*, *pasyanti*,

hinting at *para*,
the transcendent,
the sacred wood, *word*, voiced,
supreme, seen as revelation.

Finally,
unstruck melody
music of the spheres
heavenly rhapsody

choir of seraphim.
Sublimity entrancing,
exceeding *tamas*, *rajas*, *sattva*.
Going farther than every triadic formula,

the triple transformation
of physical, vital, and mental,
triggering the great eruption into vastness
unmentionable,

till the name of the rose
could be clearly grasped.
Oh, at the Hour of God,
the embrace of the Bride of the Fire!

But did she know that
for the protection she so craved,
it was hers to love, honour, and abide;
his to love, honour, and cherish,

till death did them apart.
But even death, what of it?
It was only a misnomer, mischance,
misunderstanding, born of ignorance.

For a crossing so familiar,
that each embodied being
must go back and forth over many times,
why worry?

Going as to an antechamber,
right here, right now, just as beyond the mosaic of breath
or beneath the reflection
mirroring one's face,

hidden in the hinder, nether waters.
If one knew how to dip one's hand,
thus parting the slinky surface,
like a silky surface, ever so gently,

where the subtle fault line sometimes shows,
one might slip through at least to see
and sense what those mansions of afterlife
are like.

Death is no barrier. To love each day,
learning to live experiencing
the struggle, toil, loss, but reviving
to recover our ancient selves—

that was the way of all flesh.
Thus released from our moorings,
we might roam free
in springs untramelled,

with little craving or clinging,
less conditionally,
stretching to the very stars
our self-excelling intentions.

Without fearing extinction,
proffering all that we were, are, or would be
we thus thrive and arrive
unto the ultimate cosmic reckoning.

But all this was not to be, not at all.
He had only imagined that her yawning need
signified a love so profound that death
itself could not do them apart.

Instead, he was left stranded
at the end of a world that was destroyed.
Looking back, he only saw
ruins and rubble, like a bombed out city.

The Beloved was absent,
the pain she left behind, hung low like
a poisonous fog, a miasma of regrets and longings,
choking and suffocating him.

XIX

"You live alone, don't you?" she asked.
The conversation took place
as she was checking him out.

But it was not quite a date.
He just thought he should meet others
after the *femme fatale* had dumped him.

He felt that though he was given up
for one among the dead,
he had somehow returned.

Now another woman was interested.
Was he ready, he wondered,
as he eyed at her.

She seemed the curious type,
earnestly seeking to draw him out.
Why not, he thought.

"So, do you live alone?" she repeated.
When he remained silent, she added,
"It's more an observation than a question,"

Then as if with a half apology
if not afterthought.
She persisted:

"Aren't you lonely a lot?"
He didn't know what to say,
almost as if he had forgotten to speak.

XX

Almost shyly he ventured,
"Actually, I don't live alone.
My life is peopled by many

real and imaginary beings."
"But," she countered, voice
rising a decibel, "isn't that *quite* mad?"

"Not *that* bad," he countered,
with a slight smile. "I've
seen worse and *been* worse

in the most so-called normal times."
"What do you mean? she looked worried.
"Don't you know there are people

who actually believe they're
being invaded, consumed,
about to burst or dissolve?"[15]

It was her turn to say nothing,
though she looked startled.
"These are people who hold jobs

[15] "At the deepest level people are madder than they want to believe. You will find that they fear being eaten, and are alarmed by their desire to devour others. They also imagine, in the ordinary course of things, that they will explode, implode, dissolve or be invaded," Hanif Kureishi, *Something to Tell You* (London: Faber, 2008).

raise families, run corporations
or countries, are pillars of society.
We're all far loonier, I am afraid,

than we think or care to admit."
Neither spoke for a while. Then,
he added, "It's different, you know,

living with real people as distinct
from fantastic friends or presences.
To say the least, the two modes

require dissimilar skill-sets.
But you know what's funny?
Beneath the surface, they don't

differ as much as you'd think..."
"Really! What do you mean?"
"People who live together often

have no clue about one another.
They know only a certain self
that emerges in the relationship,

thinking that to be their husband,
partner, lover, or friend.
Paired in life but parted

in death, each realises
how little they knew
not only the other

but themselves,
and each other in relationship."
"That's rather disheartening,"

she tried to be polite, striving
to keep the conversation
        alive.

"We subsist, we insist, on thinking
we are *not* alone.
But we are.

Whether we like it
        or not...."
He trailed off,

feeling forlorn,
following his own train of thought,
"All of us live alone."

XXI

"Oh," she exclaimed, "many worlds theory?"
with a rekindling of interest:
"Don't we inhabit several worlds simultaneously,

living multiple lives, not fully known to others or to ourselves?"
"Or perhaps," he returned, "who we are
is so beyond our grasp that it is only convenient

to construct an image of ourselves for the other,
to believe we know the one we claim to love."
"Does it really matter, please tell me..."

now she sounded desperate,
"to know the *real* me or you?"
(*So elusive, so alluring, so hard fought,*

he thought, *identity's last secret?*)
"The truth is, it does matter—and *doesn't*,"
he said quietly,

"Alone, together, severally—
we are as we think, our beings gossamers of imagining."
She leaned over, staring straight at him,

as if wonderstruck. He thought she was about
to kiss him. "To have and to hold," he said
instead, "is no different, ultimately,

from losing—to let go,
to let go—*all*.
Or nothing."

A hard, hateful expression
slowly formed on her overwrought face:
"So, no one will ever *entirely* possess you!"

she hissed accusingly.
"Men like you! You
are the bane of the world."

XXII

That night, again he went to bed by himself.
In his dreams, he mingled with presences
of so many dears departed,

hosts of spirits, busily humming
about their daily business,
still available for parley or palaver.

Even nastier gnomes,
ghosts, goblins, ghouls,
the apparitions and menaces of the undead.

Disturbed and terrifying,
they were still bound by laws
of conduct and character,

not free to injure and maim
at whim or will, their visiting hours
of roaming and retreat specified.

The world was given over to them
only for a certain duration.
They rambled through our realms,

trying to secure help or scare.
Sometimes he awoke exhausted,
depleted, even losing weight in his sleep.

But none could damage
or disturb him permanently.
Always we are responsible:

others can do to you only what you let them.
In the end, all was one: as below, so above.
The ancient ordinance still held.

Then, what had he really lost?
he questioned himself. After all,
he owed the delinquent dearest

the minimum concession due
from one to another human being,
though so hard to grant

to spouses or lovers lost—
to allow her
the right to let herself down,

even crash-land, if that
was what she wished.[16]

[16] "It would be wrong not to offer him the minimum respect one gave an adult, which was the option to let himself down, with a crash perhaps, if that was what he wished to do." —Jeet Thayil, *Narcopolis* (London: Faber & Faber, 2012), p. 33.

Whether traitor or
turncoat she was
free,

even if wrong in discarding him.
If this was the end, so be it,
he so schooled his soul.

Whether something else started up or not,
his faith must endure.
He was unafraid.

Identity's last secret
could never be known—or if at all known,
it could never be told.

He was not merely loved,
he was beloved
—and he was not alone.[17]

[17] "[S]omething enveloping that told her she was loved, no, beloved: she was beloved and not alone" (ibid p. 50). Thayil says this is what opium makes you feel. Is love, then, the original "opium," the only real anodyne for the unbearable pain of life, all other narcos, mere substitutes or counterfeits, having failed?

2

Yantra

Sri Yantra

A geometric, mystic symbol of creation, evolution, and

liberation, the Sri Yantra is an essential component of

worship in the Hindu Tantric system known as Sri Vidya.

The yantra consists of a set of nine interlocking triangles.

Four point upward and five downward.

They intersect to form forty-three triangles in five circles,

arranged around a central point or bindu.

The upward pointing triangles represent Shiva, the lower

ones Shakti. Conjointly, they create, sustain, dissolve,

veil, and liberate both the individual and the world.

Sri Aurobindo's Symbol

The descending triangle represents Sat-Chit-Ananda.

The ascending triangle represents the aspiring answer from matter under the form of life, light and love.

The junction of both—the central square—is the perfect manifestation having at its centre the Avatar of the Supreme—the lotus.

The water—inside the square—represents the multiplicity, the creation.

—The Mother
(https://auroville.org/contents/2855)

The yantra is, thus, a somatic-aesthetic and psycho-spiritual machine designed to manage energies, both within and around us.[18]

[18] More specifically and graphically, in Tantric traditions, the *yoni*, vagina-womb, is itself the veritable living *yantra*.

In contrast to Edvard Munch's "Love and Pain," Gustav Klimt's huge 6 x 6 ft painting, "The Kiss," shows a man passionately overpowering a woman, as she kneels before him, barefoot, face upraised, eyes closed.

Created around 1907–1908, at the height of Austria's "Golden Period," it is heavily ornamented, painted with gold leaf, silver, even platinum. Klimt's father was a gold and silver engraver.

Originally exhibited as "Liebespaar" (the lovers), it attracted immediate attention and still remains Klimt's most celebrated painting.

The man arching over the woman, has seized her upturned face with both hands.

Unshod, eyes closed almost in a trance, she submits to him.

Clinging to him, she partly clenches the tiny fingers of her right hand, hooked across his powerful neck. With her left hand, she grips his strong hands holding her face.

Do her tight, as yet unclasped hands, still show some fear, in addition to desire?

Her white face and limbs present a contrast to her swarthy, dark, and curly-haired lover. His sturdy shoulders merge into his neck in a smooth, ivory flow, as he clasps her in a virile and compelling embrace.

In the style befitting Vienna's bohemian "Golden Phase," the lovers, in their over-decorated and ornate cloaks, fuse into the floor of the flower-bed. The flat golden background profiles them almost as if they were cut-outs.

The lovers' craving is overshadowed by the embellishments and allurements of their adornments. Though, apparently in a field of flowers, they seem to be unmoving, statuesque. The kiss, still awaited, remains suspended in expectation, anticipation.

Is that how we tame or tranquilise our unbearable passions? Promising so much, what we so crave remains just that—a possibility, promise. So eagerly sought, never fully realised?

Later, exhausted, desire actually disappoints us, even descending into the trivial, sordid, or traumatic.

Gustav Klimt's "The Kiss," oil and gold leaf on canvas, Österreichische Galerie Belvedere, Vienna

Recto

In Raymond Carver's short story, "What We Talk about When We Talk about Love" There's a graphic, disturbing description of violent passion: "He beat me up one night. He dragged me around the living room by my ankles.
He kept saying, 'I love you, I love you, you bitch.' He went on dragging me around the living room. My head kept knocking on things."

The story exists in two versions, the shorter one, heavily edited by Gordon Lish, published to critical acclaim in an eponymous collection in 1981. After Carver's death in 1988, his wife, Tess Gallagher, also a writer, published the longer, original version as "Beginners" in the *New Yorker* in 2007 and later as the title story of a volume in 2009.

It is the shorter version on which Alejandro González Iñárritu bases the play within *Birdman* (2014). Carver's story itself draws on Anton Chekhov's sadly poignant tale, "About Love" (1898).

The section subtitle is inspired by Jeanette Winterson's *Why Be Happy When You Could Be Normal?* (London: Jonathan Cape, 2011). Perhaps, it might as well have been titled, "Why Be Happy When You Can Get Screwed."

Wong Kar-wai's *In the Mood for Love* (2000) suggests something of this nature:

Chow Mo-wan: In the old days, if someone had a secret they didn't want to share...you know what they did?

Ah Ping: Have no idea.

Chow Mo-wan: They went up a mountain, found a tree, carved a hole in it, and whispered the secret into the hole. Then they cover it with mud. And leave the secret there forever.

Ah Ping: What a pain! I'd just go to get laid.

Chow Mo-wan: Not everyone's like you.

In the memorable and evocative final scene of the film, Chow Mo-wan ends up whispering his secret into a hole in the mountain. The camera then cuts to a temple hall.

Did Ah Ping really love him?

The caption with which the film closes says: "He remembers those vanished years. As though looking through a dusty windowpane, the past is something he could see, but not touch. And everything he sees is blurred and indistinct."

Why Be Happy When You Can Be in Love?

I

That every piece of writing is a puzzle
is well known. Even a poem is a project
that not just tells a story or conveys a mood,
but meets a particular demand in real life.
Or finds a solution to a specific problem.

The predicament may have real-life origins
but, in writing, it devolves into tell-tale
textual trouble. Writing it out, writing *oneself*
out, that is the challenge.[19] The means.
Of be-*in*-g and be-*coming*. Of making.

Of turning a whole epic of longing
and loss into one big bang. Or at least
a shudder, gasp, groan, or whimper.
Focussing the entire passion, ache,
tenderness of a body on a single throb

or gasp. Diving into a murky pond until
one hits soft bottom. Wading through
so much sludge until one finds the elusive
amulet somewhere in the mud. *No more*,
Rushdie-like, hitting the spittoon—and *missing*.

Instead, the story's material covering, bush,
folly of woolly fuzz, has to be sheared,
trimmed, pared, to uncover the delicate,
even tender, twist in the tale—the well-oiled,
tightly coiled plot-devise. A whirring gadget,

stirring and humming, might thrash about
when roused. But it must be contained,
taken to its pinnacle, then wound down.
Taut, stiff or spun around the spindle,
the yarn must be uncoiled before it can

[19] "When it's in a book I don't think it'll hurt any more...exist any more. One of the things writing does is wipe things out. Replace them," is Marguerite Duras' oft-cited remark, whose exact source I haven't been able to find.

be woven into fabric, tactile, pliable.
Pure textile. The amorphous flux
of expectations, the sum of so many bouts,
incidents, events, details, frissons, must be
brought to a head, climaxed. That it might

abut into some definite, defined, meaningful
gesture of closure is the goal, purpose, end,
of all fiction. An exclamation if not expiry,
nonce if not nugget. Like consuming, draining,
distilling vast quantities of snitch, tosh, drivel,

twiddle, twaddle, tittle-tattle, poppycock,
claptrap, balderdash, hogwash, bunkum,
snot, before being knocked out, *knocked up,*
by a single, vital, potent, twang, plunk, plonk.
Plot: not a trick, ploy, ruse, hoax, prank, swindle,

scam, thwart, con, scumbag, or rip-off,
but the singular, sole, surviving injection,
the compelling sure shot, that breathes new life.
The solution to a great narrative challenge
thus boils down to arriving at that irreducible,

incontrovertible, iridescent, clunk, clasp, fix.
Fistful of twisted precious metal, purified,
smelted, cooled and shaped, from heaps
of ore blasted out of huge sides of rock,
dug out deep from the bowels of the earth,

in dark, smoky, and dangerous mine shafts.
At last to be curiously fashioned, yielding
something of use-value, capable of being
bought or exchanged for objects of material
utility and need in a real world. Or

at least, *at last,* a well-wrought urn,
a thing of beauty, a joy forever? Only that
is fit to be held close to one's chest, or
more curiously formed, clasped, held
in an eager, outstretched or cupped palm.

Every other exertion
is worthless self-indulgence,
wasted seed. Fit to be
carelessly shed or
merely discarded.

II

What the poet offers his mistress and ministering muse must be
a prize, a gift, a trust, produced after exacting and strenuous labour.

That accomplished, he may allow his industry some rest,
feeling he hasn't expostulated or cried out in vain.

But sometimes, the telling of a story is more of an unravelling.
Like peeling layers of onion, teary-eyed, arriving at no core.

A fruitless, tearful, *terrifying*, ordeal.
The chosen object of passion refuses to yield.

The artifice or artwork commensurate to the chief
purpose of winning her over is never accomplished.

There is no way out of the literary logjam.
The burden of the plot, the narrative responsibility,

must be dumped, else disowned. Though
so distended, it cannot be discharged.

Limping away, hobbled with dissatisfaction,
is one way of moving away after being stiffed

by the tale, *tail*. Thus one cuts one's losses,
extricating oneself from the epic fix

in which one has been snagged.
That is nearly what happened.

The poem was occasioned by difficult demands
such as Hanif Kureishi bemoans at the start

of *Something to Tell*. The lament is evocative
of the universal writerly predicament:

"Why love is difficult, sex complicated, living painful
and death so close and yet placed far away?"[20]

Doubtless, much writing, indeed great literature,
is occasioned by such questions. The poor poet,

hitched to an impossible project, has a character
to unravel who is so brave, strange, contradictory,

outrageous, incomprehensible, enraging, destructive,
destabilising, addictive, unforgettable, impassable,

impossibly compelling—that he must love
and lose her not once or twice over, but and over again..

She is the trammel that he cannot untangle,
shero-champion of a tale that resists telling.

He is strapped down, transfixed, smashed, stoned, stewed,
sloshed, wasted, ripped, bombed, blasted, buried, bereft,

[20] *Something to Tell You* (New York: Scribner, 2008).

left for dead. How to get out? How to buy his freedom
from the dungeons and dragons of writers' block-chains?

It is, he realises, the other way round,
this thousand and one nights of pain.

Scheherazade has hexed him. He must die
each night he is unable to tell his tale.

Their roles reversed, she has
the keys to the kingdom.

She holds the scimitar.
She slays him again and again.

He dies each night.
Only to be revived at dawn.

When he cannot tell his story by night,
he is condemned to be beheaded again.

Only a lesson can save him. But he
doesn't know how to learn or impart it.

He is staring at narrative collapse,
a nondescript, ignoble doom.

How to write himself out of her spell?
How to untangle truth from fancy?

The couplet comes to him with this challenge:
she is a shy bride endowed with a deadly dower.

If he cannot solve her puzzle,
he will lose her and himself be slain.

Not in any ordinary way. Tearing him apart,
she will eat him limb by limb, suck his heart out,

then discard him. Nothing strange about this.
The female praying mantis devours its mate,

just after the act, so he becomes food
not only for her fantasies, but her just fertilised

eggs. Thus the father, himself eaten,
feeds his forthcoming, about-to-hatch, offspring.

In his own case, she will eat him up
only to spit him out spitefully. Write her

he must—else she will ride, wring, and waste
him. He must figure her out or she will define him.

His fate would be to join the ranks of the reduced,
relegated, doomed, described and circumscribed.

Such is the dire distress decreed upon fruitless
psaltery. The goal and consequences of not attaining

it so clear. His script must be spare, sparse, sure,
purposeful. Overpowering, decisive, captivating,

victorious. But, instead, he is confronted by the burden
of barren vineyards and blighted fruit. Prospects of

certain ruination, insolvency, poetic bankruptcy.
His organs and instruments of inspired curiosity,

cunning or artful invention, dangle uselessly. He faces
cul-de-sacs, dead-ends, plugged-up alleys, corked

passageways, barricaded by lanes. Outlets stoppered,
scuppered, his creative cargo cannot reach its port.

It remains clogged, *clotted*, as if under embargo.
From being smitten with the character herself,

his difficulty shifts to a complication in composition,
insurmountable conundrum, knotty bundle of contrary

pulls, impulses that he cannot release, anagrams
that he cannot unravel. He is all wound up, hopelessly

entangled, ensnared, entwined, enmeshed, entrapped.
How, *who*, will emancipate him, give him his due surcease?

How will he diffuse—*defuse*—his charge? How consign
the cargo, supply, consignment, shipment? How relinquish

his responsibility, deliver the goods, drop the weight,
tender the burden of song, sense, retail, *retell*, the tale?

21 Henry Louis Vivian Derozio, the first Indian English poet, expecting little from his countrymen for all his exertions and efforts, lamented, "And let the guerdon of my labour be/My fallen country! One kind wish from thee!" ("To India My Native Land," 1828). He died young, before he was twenty-four.

III

The answer, ultimately, to all *writing* glitches is not life.
A solution that most cannot even dream of, it is *reading*.

As to his predicament, neither solve nor exit it he can,
but find the resources to overcome it he must.

It is hard labour, but in the end, *he* earns his prison break,
with the wickedest, vilest, most irreverent thoughts:

O let the guerdon of my song be one kind kick,
lick, *from thee.*[21] (Yes, click that "like" button!)

The truth was hidden in *reading*. The answer materialised
not as a consequence of the poet's punked-up personal

anguish, but the scholar-skunk's unrelated, but demanding
research. He figured the way out of the riddle that none

had deciphered. The reading pointed the way
to the writing. Writerly dilemmas had resolutions readerly.

What the reader ripped off, ripped *apart,* the writer
rapped and tapped, *typed*, out. Two parts of his

sunk, *stunk*, struck, psyche, schizoanalytically
oddballing, *spit*-balling, with one another, finally

conjoined in an act of healing, heaving, cleaving
integrating. After addling, dawdling, waddling,

coddling about for so long, he now started paddling
his skimming skiff with both oars. He was off, finally.

Lifted anchor, he set sail, leaving safer shores.
A tremendous blast of wind offered unexpected help.

It was as if an accompaniment, (un)embarrassingly
loud, letting out of air suddenly unloosed.

A fulsome fusillade, a homage, whose report
merging with its echo was heard if not smelled

for miles on end. It lighted and stank up the skies.
Up, up and away! To the high heavens themselves

mounted his benign blunderbuss,
bun-do-bust of blustering burlesque.

IV

It was the convergence of significance,
reunion he had prepared for all his life.
A long pilgrimage as to a sacred confluence.
Now suddenly he was upon it. The remedy.

When found, the answer seemed so immensely
encouraging, throbbing, pulsating, coming
as it did, with evident elegance, stark simplicity.
It becalmed him, thereupon, with quiet confidence.

Purely from the point of rhetorical prudence,
it ought not to be revealed at the outset or even
right away. It must be prepared for, curiosity
built up, suspense stoked with careful foreplay.

Narrative economy notwithstanding, besides
the temptation of instant gratification or cheap
thrills, discretion would hardly favour its
giving away cheaply, at the very outset.

Premature disclosure, if not discharge, would
certainly prove disappointing—a short-lived thrill,
unlike a long-lasting culmination. The secret spent,
given away too soon or cheaply, even before asked,

let alone awaited with bated breath, who would read on?
On the other hand, the argument unstated, unintroduced
made for a bad commencement. As token of a writer's
earnestness, wouldn't it be only fair to offer a foretaste

of the main course? Aren't we all in the gist business?
Shouldn't the gentle reader decide whether to leave
or stick it out till the end? The jury is still out on the most
expedient strategy. Narratives matter. Only that much

is true. When it comes to storytime, who cares for
the too too cautious? Don't tell all right away. No point
stuffing it in the face. Hold back after revealing only
so much, a bit of tantalising bait, so as to hook the reader.

Once impelled, no one can resist the issue. Signal received,
he had to push on compelled, regardless of the outcome.
Ensnared, entrapped, propelled, his course set,
there was no going back. Deep down in his bones he knew,

but never cared to admit or acknowledge the fact,
that writing comes from writing, not from life. Words
come out from other words not from experiences.
It's a bit like money. It comes from, *of*, money, not

labour, work, business, commerce, trade, or industry.
But bringing words out of words is not as easy
as it sounds. It is not only talent you need, but lots
of effort. You must have a real appetite for the work.

It takes over your life, interferes with all other plans,
messes with the daily business of living—even
eating, sleeping, shopping, working, fornicating
is addicting. It can get you high, but also pull

you down. It is lonely. It is dangerous. It's what you
live for. At least when it comes. That is all you do,
that is all you are. Better accept it. There is
no escape from it. In telling his story each writer

has to acknowledge his debts. Especially to texts
that helped him resolve his narrative distress.
Not just to write his way out, but write it all up.
Also, actually to understand what that entailed,

what was really at stake. In the process, the text
started in one fashion, is finished off in another.
A shift, a turn, a change of directions ensues
somewhere along the way. Without such recalibration,

the tale is sure to flounder. But an unexpected
convolute reveals the clandestine nugget. Surprise!
The tragedy transforms into a screw-up, *screwball.*
Threnody to a comic farce to burlesque....Wait!

That is not all. In third part, a Tantra, retelling
an ancient myth, presents itself. What is going on?
Hit or miss, *ms.*, or amiss? If the first got him started,
the second brought him to a head. If he had not

discovered the third, he would not have dared
to enter the secret, *sacred,* wood, inside the thicket.
He put his finger in what at first resembled a beehive.
He was stung, smarting horribly. The second showed

how to exit the snatch. Eureka! He found the honey
and dipped his tongue in it. Because he was ensnared,
he ventured to find the trapdoor. Without being enrapt,
he could not have pushed onward to the unravelling,

bringing his plot to its clinch. What followed
was a synch—all the way from the spasm
to the endless cards cascade, the gushing climax
and conclusion of his protacted game of solitaire.

Tantra restored the balance. Tranquillity.
From *c✿ntempt* to *c✿ntainment* to *c✿ntentment.*
What after that? Only *c✿ntemplation*? Looking back,
what seemed typical, standard to any serious exercise

of art, was unlike anything he'd ever experienced or expressed.
These intertexts were not tricks, but tremors. Shocks, shudders,
that shifted him out of his torpor and turgidity. Not merely
devices, artifices, curlicues, utterly lacking in *conviction*—

they appeared miraculously, out of absolute
necessity. They rang true, moaning *convincingly.*
He felt the faith he'd never before
encountered. An exhilaration of discovery

to *convey*. He had solved the mystery,
overcome his *confusion*. That was
the wonder of the vision, the truth of the telling. He could
not be certain, but he must go for it.

Thar she blows![22] as plainly as possible. The enigma
of arrival, of coming, encapsulated in a terse testimonial.
Like letters written in light during the toil and turmoil
of the darkest night. Tenuous. Tentative. Then certain—

there could be no return, no going back. Only renewal.
Going forward. As far as he was concerned, he was done.
He had found what he was after. He was finished.
Tamam shud, consummatum est.

V

Binoy Majumdar, poet-who-went-mad, started
differently.[23] His book wasn't at first called
Phire Esho Chaka, roughly, "Come back Chaka,"
where *Chaka* referred to his heroine's name.

"*Chaka*"—what kind of a name is that? Wait.
Be patient. But here's the clue.
He'd first called his book simply, *Gayatrike*,
"For Gayatri," dedicating it to an impossible love.

But a year later, he reissued it under the modified
title, *Phire Esho Chaka.* As I've already confessed,
unlike Binoy, I was led elsewhere, to someplace else.
That's how my poem became, by mistake, a—

dash—or *slash.* It exposed her true face. A *gash*?
Was *that* her secret? Unspeakable, unmentionable,
Was it a stubborn silence that was at the heart
of the matter? It resisted revealing. Where was

the art that could show the path to *twat* thicket
or *twat Tathata*?[24] Then what of the plot?
Phire esho meant *turn back*—but I'd already
grasped there could be no *return.* Only *renewal.*

[22] The hail of the whaling lookout, made famous in Herman Melville's *Moby Dick* (1851).

[23] The Sahitya Akademi award winning poet, whose posthumous fame is growing, was a pioneer of "Hungry" poetry (https://scroll.in/article/1005607/how-binoy-majumdar-re-wrote-the-grammar-of-dalit-poetry-and-politics-and-was-ostracised-for-it). Spivak spells his name as "Binay." I have preferred the more standard "Binoy."

[24] *Twat*, also meaning a stupid or annoying person, may be pronounced, wherever necessary, as *"that"* in this section. *Tathata* is a Sanskrit word and key concept in Mahayana Buddhism meaning "such-ness or thus-ness," the ultimate nature of phenomenal reality. "In its very origin suchness is of itself endowed with sublime attributes. It manifests the highest wisdom which shines throughout the world, it has true knowledge and a mind resting simply in its own being. It is eternal, blissful, its own self-being and the purest simplicity; it is invigorating, immutable, free... Because it possesses all these attributes and is deprived of nothing, it is designated both as the Womb of Tathagata and the Dharma Body of Tathagata."—Thomas Berry, *Religions of India: Hinduism, Yoga, Buddhism* (New York: Columbia University Press, 1996), p. 170. It may be noted that "*tat*" (Sanskrit) and "*that*" (English) are cognates.

Going forward. Had Binoy realised that? But like Binoy,
I, too, did not know much about this till later. After
all the pain was over and done with, halfway into
my trans-genre text, I became slowly, dimly, painfully,

prescient—aware that there could be *no return*.
Phire esho would not work. She would never
come back, return as Binoy so hoped and desired.
It was, moreover, not the solution to the existential

situation or narrative puzzle. There was another
far riskier, more dangerous route to take. Few
ever ventured on it for it could prove fatal. What
was this way? How did I stumble upon it?

It was by way of the blood trail that led to the gap,
the gash, the wound.[25] To *twat*, *through twat*, I found
the way. *Twat* was the solution to the real—and narrative—
conundrum. So the journey of this work, which is

also the story of its composition, was from the clues
afforded in one text to the red trail revealed in another.
The writer had to turn back, *phire* āsā, into critic or best
reader. How else to appreciate the literature we admire

than *write*, critically engaging with it? Isn't that the way
to show how much we care, how much it matters to us?
This, then, is the third and middle path, which combines both
the creative and critical, joining writing with reading.

It is a form of translation, turning one thing into another.
Literary as well as cultural carrying over, carrying across,
in which primary text ceases to be itself to be reborn in another
tongue. "Translating into English" is, in fact, the commonest

form of interpretation these days. But an essay by that name
by a famous critic conceals within the cocoon of high theory
the tragic tale of the demented poet, Binoy, mentioned,
invoked, and recalled many times: *phire esho, Binoy-da.*

With its uncommon form of a poetry followed by essay,
followed by poetry again, or criticism sandwiched
between poems or theory, *poetics,* which combines both,
this composition, in many footnotes, admits its major debts.

Gayatri Chakravorty Spivak and Jeanette Winterson:
one a critic-theorist-translator, the other a fiction writer.
Knowing Professor Spivak slightly and Winterson not
at all, a good place to start would be with the former.

[25] On 29 May 2014, performance artist, Deborah de Robertis, exposed her vagina in front of Courbet's L'Origine du Monde (Origin of the World) at the Musée d'Orsay. Her live performance of "Mirror of Origin" was interrupted by museum security and staff who evicted her and cheering visitors from the premises. Explaining her stance, de Robertis said, "There is a gap in art history, the absent point of view of the object of the gaze. In his realist painting, the painter shows the open legs, but the vagina remains closed. He does not reveal the hole, that is to say, the eye. I am not showing my vagina, but I am revealing what we do not see in the painting, the eye of the vagina, the black hole, this concealed eye, this chasm, which, beyond the flesh, refers to infinity, to the origin of the origin" (https://news.artnet.com/exhibitions/artist-enacts-origin-of-the-world-at-musee-dorsay-and-yes-that-means-what-you-think-35011).

VI

The title of this book, *Identity's Last Secret*, comes from the twelfth chapter, "Translating into English," of Spivak's *Aesthetic Education in an Era of Globalization*.[26]

Of her twenty-plus tomes, it is *Aesthetic Education* that is perhaps the most deeply felt and moving. The harvest of a quarter century of enunciation and performance, it actively pursues "a distracted theory...of the double bind" (ix).

Spivak claims she has found the solution to double-binds in the *suggestion* that "the humanities can somehow learn to resolve double binds by playing them" (ibid).

In the very middle of the book, at its heart as it were, is this essay, "Translating into English." And the last third of this essay grapples with Spivak's "particular ambivalence"—or should I say double bind?—in *playing* an extraordinary collection of poems.

This is the volume that poses a special challenge to her. Why should that be, when she has, with easy expertise, casual, sometimes caustic, competence, disposed of several better known, not to speak of much more difficult, texts?

Why is this book at once exciting and exacting for Spivak, both as reader-critic and translator-subject?

The answer is at once strange and startling. Unlike any other, it is in reading this slim volume of poems that "she makes the mistake of thinking the named subject is she" (273).

The collection in question is by the "mad" poet Binoy Majumdar (1934–2006). It was first published in 1961, the year Gayatri, not yet twenty, left for the United States.

It's original title, which few know, was simply *Gayatrike*—to Gayatri, as has already been mentioned.

The following year, the book reissued as *Phire Esho Chaka*, was known subsequently by this title. Which is why it bears closer attention. Though often translated as "Come Back, O Wheel," Spivak herself leaves out "O," rendering it as the rather unpoetic, "Come Back Wheel."

Spivak, after all, is a terrible translator. Or to put it more politely, she is a much better critic than translator. Even as latter, it is owing to the former's skills that she really makes her singular and stellar contribution.

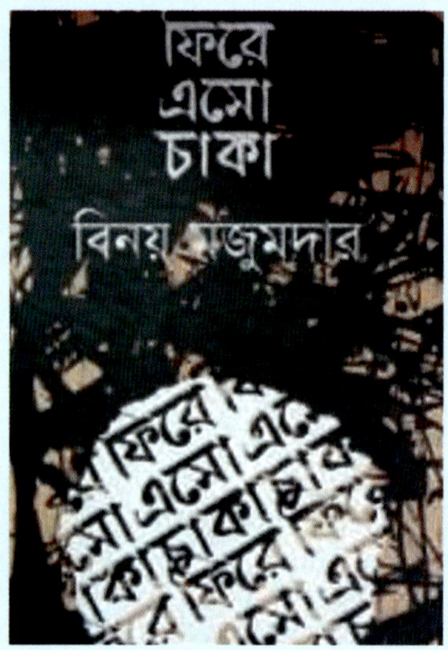

The cover of the 51-page reprint of *Phire Esho Chaka* by Kobi Prokashoni, Kolkata, in 2011

[26] Published by Harvard University Press in 2012, the chapter in question is found from pp. 256–274. An earlier version of the same chapter appeared in Sandra Bermann and Michael Wood, eds., *Nation, Language and the Ethics of Translation* (Princeton, NJ: Princeton University Press, 2005): 93–110.

Phire has the sense of turn, so "turn back," with the feel of both coming and returning, might work better. Indeed, there is a poem in the volume which suggests as much, albeit more in the sense of turning away than turning back:

> What is needed is a sudden turn
> leaving the swift hand that plucks butterflies out of the air
> gaping at a loss.
> The others exist pale and ghostly as stars
> brought to brief life by a total eclipse of the sun.
> But I cannot change my course now; can the leopard
> unspin its leap in mid-air?
> Moreover, they may still be wrong. She can yet appear.
>
> (Translated by Jyotirmoy Datta)[27]

The poet, hoping against hope, yearns for his Gayatri's return, although he—and the others—are mistaken in believing that she won't. She will, but not in the expected manner, as I shall show.

But the jilted lover is not an entirely deluded poet. As another poem makes it amply clear, he knows she will not come back:

> I have given up strewing grain on the ground
> to have the birds join me at lunch.
> Only when the baby is cut adrift
> does it have its free hunger and thirst;
> like taking off a blindfold to be confronted with
> a curtain, being born
> into this vast uterus, lined with a sky porous with stars.
>
> (Translated by Jyotirmoy Datta)

Spivak glosses her translation of the title thus: "The Sanskrit *chakra* of the surname means wheel and is transformed into *chaka* in modern Bengali. A cunning translation" (271).

Again, Spivak is only partly right.

"*Chaka*" here serves as a pun, not translation: a double-entendre, it refers both to wheel and to Spivak herself. This she neglects to tell.

Why would she, or anyone, link the title to her surname?

Because the book, despite its changed name, is dedicated to Gayatri Chakravorty.

Speaking of herself in the third person, Spivak explains: "Chakravorty did not know the poet, although she had noticed the intensity of his gaze" (271).

Against this, is the testimony of the poet, unreliable though it might be, appearing in a Foreword of a reprint over forty years later:

> This book of poems, focused on a girlfriend, and dealing only with a plea for love is indeed a diary....If you think only of me, this poetry is only a plea for love....Yet, because any one part is applicable to many situations connected to love, social theory, politics, science and many other topics, therefore one should be able to find a successful realisation of any kind of situation in the lives of any sort of reader, male or female. (271)

In alluding to Spivak's reading of this collection, it is time to underscore and celebrate how Majumdar's prediction—or wish—has indeed come true.

Binoy has, arguably, at last found a "successful realisation" to his fervent wish, denied to him during his lifetime. His lady love has deigned to look, if not at him, at least at his poems. She has even *translated* some of them.

This is the sort of upheaval that I have myself tried to contend with in this very book.

Majumdar's collection, *Phire Esho Chaka,* enjoyed a brief revival, partly as a result of the international fame of she to whom it was dedicated.

[27] This and the following translation are from http://www.kaurab.com/english/bengali_poetry/binoy.html

No wonder, it was about his putative connection with Spivak that the poet was asked repeatedly.

In his slim, *Complete Works*, Spivak finds a letter written in 1992, setting the record straight:

> Gayatri Chakravorty was a student at Presidency College, and came First Class First in English in her B.A., in 1960 or 1961 A.D. [actually 1959]. Thinking that she alone would understand my poems the book, *To Gayatri*, was addressed to her, and therefore I called the book *To Gayatri*, and I wrote in the book what I had to say to her.[28]

Majumdar seems deliberately to have underlined the relation of the poems to Spivak, first by naming the collection after her, then changing the title to an indirect, but unmistakeable allusion but retaining the dedication to her inside its covers, and, finally, by returning the book to its original title, *Gayatrike*, in his complete works.

Could there be any doubt that the poet, with such unambiguous naming and re-naming, intended his connection with his Gayatri to be unknown or even disguised?

In an earlier interview given in 1986, when asked, "Were you in love with Gayatri?" Binoy replies:

> Hey, no—I only knew her for two or three days—she was a famously beautiful student of English literature at Presidency College—then she went off somewhere—to America or someplace, I'm not sure. Then why write poems about her? One must write about someone, after all. Can one write forever about mango trees, jackfruit trees, and tuberoses?[29]

As this early photo shows, Spivak was "famously beautiful." Despite Binoy's disclaimers, the editor of the reprint, Kanakabati Dutta, cannot help but think that "there is some connection," not only in Binoy's erotic one-sided poetic fascination for Gayatri, but also between Binoy's "perceptive glance" and Spivak's "spreading Derrida."

Perhaps out of excessive kindness, not utterly dismissive of this unlikely claim, Spivak politely remarks, "Perhaps there's something there."

Aside from Dutta's wrong dates—Spivak reminds us that she started teaching Derrida, Lacan, and Foucault in the 1960s, not the 1980s (561)—there is no disproof, let alone reproof.

How might Binoy have influenced Gayatri to take up, *take on*, Derrida?

What could the poet's hopeless and obsessive gaze have to do with Spivak's reading, translating, teaching, and generally "spreading" Derrida?

That and whatever else might have been, notwithstanding how preposterous these possibilities, is left to our imagination.

Spivak not only departed from Kolkata for the US in 1961, she never even read Majumdar's poems for decades, "although she knew the fame of the book, and that it was dedicated to her" (271).

Twice in the essay she asserts: "There is no question of response" (271, 272), "other than what you read here" (271).

A disclaimer that seems unnecessary in a book published in 2012 when the poet is already dead? But the caution was probably still needed in 2005, when the essay first appeared in print.

28 "Phire Esho Chakar Nam Paribartan Shommondhe," *Kabyoshamogro*, 1 (Kolkata: Pratibhash, 1993): 162, cited in Spivak 561.

29 Spivak wonders whether the poet's reference to the "mango trees, jackfruit trees, and tuberoses" requires interpretation, but passes on after hinting that she might attempt one later. To me, the size and progression, from mangoes, jackfruit, to tuberoses, suggests process, ripening, death: the mango is a smaller, breast-shaped fruit; the jackfruit, much larger, suggesting a full womb; tuberoses are often offered at funerals. But, I am being fanciful here.

Spivak's photo is from https://hungryderphoto.wordpress.com/2017/12/11/binoy-majumdars-muse-gayatri-chakraborty/

Spivak justifies her earlier, decades-long indifference to Binoy's poetic, if not pathetic, fixation:

> Many of the poems lament her absence, his loneliness without a response. It is not clear that such lamentations, included in poetry, require "response" in the ordinary way. Must the lost object not remain lost for the poems to retain their exact verbal contour? (272)

This is the crux, *double bind,* that makes our two texts intertwine.

VII

Doubtless, Binoy's poems, with their repeated identification of the person addressed, were pleas for some consideration.

But what kind of response could be given?

Spivak suggests that the poems themselves would have somehow failed if they had actually made it extra-textually, as love letters or appeals for attention, drawing the Gayatri of flesh and blood into the poet's net of ardour.

The loss of the wished-for object is the precondition, according to Spivak, of the very substance, if not success, of the poems.

That is why Spivak, it would seem, is more concerned with the "problems of entering the protocols of a text" (271) than with what happens to the poet in real life.

For sure, she has enforced a protocol that will strictly prevent him from entering her life in any way.

She reports with clinical objectivity, almost as a matter of fact, bordering on indifference, that the poet went "mad"—and died.

A photograph from those harrowing times might be worth a thousand words.

(http://www.kaurab.com/english/bengali_poetry/binoy.html)

Perhaps Spivak was afraid that during his lifetime, any reaction other than what she offered as a critic, might actually exacerbate the poet's illness.

But, as we know, the reprint forty years later in 2002, is even more insistent. Binoy turns turtle, restoring the title from *Phire Esho Chaka* back to the much more direct and unambiguous *Gayatrike*—to Gayatri.

Isn't his entreaty for some, *any*, attention from his addressee even more urgent now? Or is it the recklessness of defeated desire? But Spivak, the object of his affections, again, resolutely says: "There is no question of response. The occasion of these poems has been translated into the transcendental" (272).

The poems, in other words, have been occasioned by nothing real, nothing material, nothing to do with Spivak; the poet *imagined* it all. Thus, no response is called for or possible.

Yet, despite such a repudiation, Spivak cannot help reading the poems in a somewhat more personal way, relating some lines not so much to herself as to the real, not so transcendental, experiences of the poet, who was "in and out of mental hospitals for the last forty-odd years of his life" (272).

After all, "there are poems that delicately hint how 'madness' must be managed: 'I will now be mad, at last by insane claws I/ Will prise out the angel's home address, the door'" (ibid).[30]

In the light of the poet's sad demise and a last narrative poem, not included in the original publication of 1961, Spivak's cryptic remark on how the "occasion of these poems has been translated into the transcendental" acquires a special poignancy.

Binoy, in that supplementary poem, actually imagines that he and his "Dream Girl" will be united in heaven after their deaths, but in still youthful and real bodies.

In that afterlife, his divine mistress (*amar ishwari,* as he addresses her), reminiscent of Beatrice to Dante, "promises that she will spend...an eternity of shared conjugal life" (274) with the poet whom she had ignored so completely all his living years.

His unrequited love has its only fulfilment in the projected afterlife in which both poet and muse, Binoy and Gayatri, are *translated* to heaven.

If so, do Binoy's poems, lamentations as Spivak dubs them, cry for her kindness in the real world?

Or is the very opposite their demand? If the lost object were found, wouldn't the very raison d'etre of the work flounder?

"Note from the Underground" (for the diligent reader):

Doesn't my text, too, demand a real response from
a real person? But if it were ever forthcoming,
would that not negate its very reason for being?
More intriguingly, what if the universe responds,

not in terms of the intended or expected addressee?
Actually, what Identity's Last Secret *proves, is*
that the universe does answer. With another, sometimes,
even more fulfilling mantra or mode of attainment?

Let us, however, return to the unrequited love story of Binoy and Spivak.

Spivak has been inflexibly unsentimental so far, refusing to identify with the person addressed, the person the collection is dedicated to.

Though she has repudiated any easy or flattering identification with the person of her name to whom the poems have been dedicated, she still hopes, with another sort of possessiveness that "they will not be translated soon" *because* "at last I would like to translate them" (272).

No one else will translate these poems, but she must—because she is, somehow, implicated in them. Again, she is

30 The opposite of Lear: "O let me not be mad, not mad, sweet heaven! I would not be mad. Keep me in temper, I would not be mad" (I.5.43–44), a resemblance which Spivak fails to notice?

vain or plain wrong. Others, indeed, have translated Binoy's poems. In fact, his "sacrifice" won him the Sahitya Akademi award the year before his death.

Playing with her double bind—is it albatross or crow—she has still found a way out, not as the poet's lover or heavenly mistress, but as his earthly translator and literary partner.

She is especially taken, in the process of such a preliminary translation as offered in the essay, with the poems' auto-erotic textuality, especially the poet's "repeated references" to himself as "a letter lying on the wrong threshold, destined to err":

> Come and pick me up like torn bits of a letter
> Put 'em together for curiosity's sake, read once and leave
> As if to disappear, leaving them like a slant look. (272)

Again, we see Spivak's inadequacy as translator—wouldn't "askance" or even "slanted" have worked better than "slant"?

But Binoy, her poet-lover, himself would never agree. What does it matter if someone else can translate him better? It is only Gayatri he desires; her holding him in her arms, even if only textually after his death, is bliss. Especially after keeping him at arm's length for so long.

As translator if not lover, hasn't she picked up the torn bits of the mangled body of the poet's one-sided, doomed love, turning his pleas back to poems, giving their disintegrated and scattered fragments the purpose and direction of a letter which has finally reached its cherished destination, thus allowing herself as their translator, to be conquered not by the poet's love, but by the irresistibility of his poetic intention?

Yet is her posthumous healing touch unfinished, as is her double bind itself unresolved. The poems have not yet found their real translator, only the intended one.

Spivak, after all, has offered but a sampler, quoting a few lines, translating only some of the poems.

After preaching so much against transcendence and advocating so strenuously the imperative to de-transcendentalise, Spivak cannot alter her equation with the text: "I am the figure of the girl, the translator thinks, making that easy mistake, and this book offers what the poet sees as he casts his net. I come up both ways, albatross and crow. This is a lesson: to enter the protocols of a text one must other its characters" (274).

But isn't she too late? The poet is already translated to heaven. He is dead; there is no longer any danger of any physical contact or *contamination*. Spivak, the atheist, cannot believe in any sort of afterlife. But what of the afterlife of texts in translation?

Gayatri, Binoy's "Dream Girl" and *ishwari*, has owned up a few of the poems addressed to her by translating them into English.

But the dead poet's unfulfilled love remains trapped in pages of poetry, restless and full of mourning, just as the collection itself remains untranslated.

No peace here or in the hereafter?

The *chaka* cannot turn back; the poems dedicated to Gayatri will remain never fully owned up or acknowledged.

And as to a heavenly reunion, its prospects too must remain one-sided.

Sadly, Spivak has approached the poem only as an(y) other reader would—with no special empathy or identification.

But then, almost unintentionally, she betrays herself.

Deny as she might that she has nothing to do with the addressee of Binoy's poems, that she is just another reader, not the object of the poet's affections, she proves herself wrong.

How?

By becoming not *just* another, *any*, reader, but special kind of reader. Not just critic, but *translator*.

What do translators do? They transport meaning. In this case, the dead poet's words come alive in another language, conveyed by the very lady love who had spurned him all along.

Through translation, at last she owns up, requiting and recompensing Binoy for all the earthly neglect that she meted out to him.

The poet is already dead, *translated.*

By translating his words, she *de*-transcendentalises him.

One translation undoes the other; the dead poet is brought back to an afterlife, as Benjamin prophesied, in another language.

Having rejected Binoy during his life, Spivak translates, *embraces*, him after his death back to an afterlife.

Almost in spite of herself, reader becomes translator: every act of translation is an act of betrayal, after all—*traduttore traditore.*

In this case, Spivak betrays not Binoy, but herself. She is now untrue to her own earlier indifference. She acknowledges and pays attention to Binoy's poems.

In "translating into English" Binoy's Bangla poems dedicated to her, Spivak betrays not so much the "original" text or even Binoy. Rather, she betrays the person addressed in the poems, *herself* the "original" the love-object of the poems.

She has, through translation, accepted the poems addressed to her. Not as poet's real-life beloved or object of desire, but as his textual bride, re-birthing them in another tongue.

Spivak's refusal to be seduced by the text is revealed, at last, to be only partially successful.

Similarly, her attempt to resurrect the poet, bring him back to life, albeit in another tongue, too, succeeds only partially. Her translations are not good enough, both in terms of their quality and quantity.

The poet remains neither there, nor here.

Spivak too, now neither rejecting him completely, nor owning him up after his death, remains in her double-bind.

What with the poet's wished for fulfilment remaining transcendent, while his beloved critic-translated persists in atheistic insistence on othering and de-transcendentalising it both textually and sexually.

Her play remains just that. A play. A ploy. A plot. Neither failure nor success.

VIII

One of the unintended consequences of Spivak's engagement with Binoy's work is that it invites comparison with another text. Its author was much more fortunate. At least in actually getting the girl in question.

I refer to Talbot Spivak. Gayatri's first husband. She married him when she was just twenty-four. Divorced thirteen years later in 1977, she still retains his surname. Which is why I refer to her throughout not as Gayatri, as Binoy did, but as Spivak.

Talbot was Gayatri's fellow-student at Cornell. Like Binoy, he too was deeply touched by her. But instead of a book of poems, he published a novel. Just one. *The Bride Wore the Traditional Gold* (New York: Knopf, 1972). It fictionalises a part of their life together.

Long out of print, the text is rather difficult to get. On Amazon, stray copies are still offered, but at extortionate prices. I found one priced at $343.

Arguably, even understandably, its connection with Gayatri, how she is portrayed, is its foremost, if not only, interest today.

When published, it had a small, somewhat mixed reception. A note in *Kirkus Reviews* observed: "The tone is nice, the prose style clear and simple, but the structure is marred by the inclusion of trivial lists and conversations culled from the author's seventy notebooks, which seem a cop-out for genuine re-creation of the past."

Even then, before Gayatri was an international celebrity, it is her presence that illuminates the book. The half-Jewish Philadelphian narrator is simply besotted by her.

The narrative is driven by his "ongoing love affair with his Brahmin (B.A. at sixteen) wife." (Actually, it should have been B.A. at *seventeen* if Gayatri *is* its original inspiration.)

Does that alone make for worthwhile reading rather than the "very intricate (or interesting) byways of the author's mind"?

In the novel, the character modelled on Gayatri teaches not high theory, feminism, or Marxism—but Sanskrit!

A Brahmin who teaches Sanskrit, the very anti-thesis of the Marxist-Materialist-Feminist-Post-colonialist Spivak the world knows?

Wait, there's more.

The narrator, as it happens, is constantly "worrying about her possible affair ... with a middle-aged mediocre poet."

But oh! could that possibly be a reference to poor Binoy Majumdar? Was he a private joke in the young couple's courtship and romance?

That would go counter to the stoutness with which she has denied any real contact with him in *Aesthetic Education.*

The *Kirkus* reviewer knows nothing of Binoy's plight, though.

Peregrine Wingfield's comment, aside from the *Kirkus* notice, is perhaps more to the point, if not none the less incisive:

> Very witty, touching novel by Gayatri Spivak's first husband. Hard to guess that the petty fascist he describes would turn out to be one of America's leading radical intellectuals. The girl in the novel sounds like a petty bourgeois tramp, fresh off the boat from Calcutta, armed with a fake BBC accent and a thoroughly screwed up personality. Perhaps it's all fiction, but anyone wanting a glimpse of Gayatri Spivak "at home" should read this (https://www.amazon.com/bride-wore-traditional-gold/dp/0394472853)

We have too high a regard for Spivak to be persuaded by such a scurrilous putdown.

But we cannot help remembering that Spivak has been pilloried in one more novel, Rukun Advani's *Beethoven among the Cows* (New Delhi: Ravi Dayal, 1994).

A famous, oft-quoted jibe runs: "Professor [Lavatri] Alltheorie's *Collected Marxist Phonecalls* had outsold *Gone with the Wind*... Her *Collected Feminist Faxes* was in press. Her opponents defined her subject-position with a law—Lavatri's Law: Incredible Articulation + Incredible Incomprehension = Incredible Salary."

The character based on Spivak actually appeared earlier in 1993 as "Professor Lavatri Lavatory Spewhack." Printed in a slim booklet called *Indian History from Above and Below*, it was published from Lucknow by Rukun's father, Ram Advani, a respected bookseller, the proprietor of a well-frequented bookshop in Hazratganj.

One of the parodies in it, "History from Below," appeared in the *Statesman* earlier as *Hiss and Tell: The Loud Ladies' Journal*. Rukun spoofs Spivak's famous essay "Can the Subaltern Speak" as "Can the Subaltern *Squeak*?" (emphasis added).

Here, then, is the double bind of love, such as all of us find ourselves in at one time or the other. Our love can never be translated—or following Spivak, *de-transcendentalised*—into reality.

Binoy's "Dream Girl" must remain a dream, confined to the pages of poetry, never walking out of his text into reality.

Poetry remains poetry.
It is never incarnated in flesh.
Except in a theological sense.
Likewise, love fully requited
and reciprocal remains a dream.
Never fulfilled in the here and now,
it is always postponed to the never-ever
of the hereafter. And yet, here and now,
can we stop loving? Just as we cannot
give up dreaming just because dreams
are impossible to realise.
(Isn't revolution itself one such dream?)

Spivak, then, inspires poems and novels of love, reciprocated or otherwise.

Also a campus romance, which in real-life abuts into marriage, but ends in divorce.

And, much later, a rather merciless satire, from "above and below."

The girl to whom the poem is addressed, whether Binoy's Gayatri—or Spivak's love interest—never (re)turns.

Nor does the difficult paramour of *Identity's Last Secret*, whose tortuous tale I've told thus far.

Only in words can such Muses
be secured or tethered, never in life.
Entrammelled in text, but lost
in real life, the heroine becomes
a blur on the horizon of memory,
leaving only a wound, a rent,
a gap, in the fabric of desire.

The poem remains just that, a poem.
Even when itself translated
into a missive, plea, or petition,
with a real "intended" or beloved
as its addressee or love object.
Because the latter never responds,
returns, to the poet or requites his love.

IX

Ever so early in our courtship,
my mistress, for that is how
she called and classed herself
—"*Dominatrix of all your organs
and senses*"—dissed my interest

in theory, my many papers
even books on the subject,
not to mention its high priestess,
Gayatri Chakravorty Spivak.
"*Theory,* did you say?

I have no use for it.
It's never moved me.
Spivak is a Bong who went bonkers.
Imagine, she could have
been another Tagore or Ray,

but became Ms Theory-Feary
instead. What a loss."
She mocked the craze for
incomprehensibility: "It's all
so arid. I don't get goosebumps

reading Foucault or Derrida.
Vagueology cannot challenge or puzzle
as poetry does." It could not drown her
in pools of passion or poison.
It did not demand of her

to delve below the surface,
to tease out its sense.
Certainly, it would not give her
the sensuous rapture
of a lover's caress:

"I need to feel it here, in the pit
of my stomach. It should hit
me there." But she pointed carelessly
a little lower than the abdomen,
then remarked wistfully:

"How wonderful it would be
to be the woman Neruda or Faiz loved,
to know that all those poems
were written only for me..."
Listening to her words

I found a rising tide of hurt,
even envy: wasn't *I* a poet too?
Why did only Neruda or Faiz count?
Why was I excluded from the reckoning,
bypassed, *expelled*, from the ranks

of passionate pilgrims of ardour and loss?
Did she never consider that I might write
her poems if not as grand,
then at least passably good?
Why would I never fulfil

her need, her longing to be loved,
adored and immortalised in verse?
As if to make up for this lack,
I determinedly wrote a series of poems.
Later that year, just before she left,

went bad, on Christmas Day, she messaged:
"What is there to show for our years together?
There is nothing particular that you
were able to give me. Nothing at all."
Then, as if by way of an afterthought,

wryly warming up to her theme:
"Ah, I know you're writing a book.
I know it'll be terribly damning.
You'll portray me as a crazed bitch...
But, tell me, are you really a *poet?*

You'll publish even your laundry list,
no? So what of these poems,
compositions, as you call them, who will
bother to read them? Who cares for
your scribblings, your *execrations*?"

She chortled in full-throated spite.
"But," making light of her indignities,
I returned, "aren't we forgetting
something? Only poems stand
between you, me and lunacy."

Even if they pass unnoticed in the marketplace of letters,
they will still be real. Their existence will not be denied.
One day they will resurface, not in helpless bitterness,
but resurrected from the grave, recast in new bodies,
endowed with wings, clothed in heavenly raiment.

Light, translucent, they will fly, reborn, *translated,*
free. Would I, I however wondered ruefully, really
excoriate her, anathemising her hold on my soul,
like a curse? Would I wash our *dirty linen* in poems
she'd so demeaned by calling them my *laundry list*?

I suddenly understood something that had eluded me
till then. True, our relationship had an aura of unreality.
But these poems had an existence of their own. That even she
couldn't deny. Perhaps, poetry would redeem
both of us and itself, even as the complete collapse

and failure of our relationship couldn't be averted.
Now, when she is no longer in my world,
the multiple, mutual benefits of the rupture become obvious.
When there's nothing left to impress upon her,
I can also write this strange book, including

the burlesque this is the record of my great
derangement. It must not be denied or airbrushed.
It may not be the kind of work she or
other readers relish let alone respect, but
it remains my requiem to grand failures.

Consider it a useless extravagance like my love,
just *baje khoroch*, its purpose never realised,
giving itself in vain, spending itself without
recompense. Trampled, stamped upon,
kicked out and crushed repeatedly, love,

once again up-rears its tiny, timid,
oh-so-green head from the black sodden earth.
So uncertainly, it glances about the world
of men. It is yet to learn to be afraid
of failure, even of death.

Born again, content anew just to be,
just to love, it asks for nothing more,
nothing else. Crushed and ground down
again and again, it cannot be rooted out,
fully extirpated, eradicated, exterminated.

These lines had stopped me in my tracks.
I did not know how to go on.
I had reached the *Na Hanyate* moment,
to invoke another star-crossed love story
that turned into fiction.

Maitreyi Devi's rejoinder,
nay counter-narrative,
to Mircea Eliade's perfidy,
the violation of her innocence in
La Nuit Bengali (*Bengal Nights*).

Isn't that sort of transcendental move,
at the very point that reality bites,
becomes excruciating, almost
the obligatory evasion? Isn't poetry
escapist rather than victorious?

Lacking the credibility or resonance
of the ancient proclamation, a verse might
claim success in the hereafter as much
as one likes. But when we had failed here
and now, who would believe us?

My move smacked too much of a loser's
face-saving hideaway, a compensation
that does not count, actually a step-down
rather than step-up. Therefore a failure
both *vyavaharic* and *adhyatmic*, material

and spiritual, twice inadequate, double
defeat after double trouble, not twin triumph.
As Swami Vivekananda had warned,
this was the typical defeated Hindu's
tamas masquerading as *sattva*.[31]

Perhaps, all I had accomplished
was to offer my own version
of sad Binoy's story
of fully failed love and
partially successful poetry.

Something *was* lost in translation.
Identity's last secret
still remained unrevealed.
The story was unfinished,
but the clue to its completion

lay elsewhere. Where was it
locked away? Spivak didn't have
the answer. "Translating into English"
failed to provide the way
out of the labyrinth.

[31] "Do you think that a man who does not exert himself at all, who only takes the name of Hari, shutting himself up in a room, who remains quiet and indifferent even when seeing a huge amount of wrong and violence done to others before his very eyes, possesses the quality of Sattva? Nothing of the kind, he is only enshrouded in dark Tamas. How can the people of a country practice religion who do not get even sufficient food to appease their hunger?" (https://www.ramakrishnavivekananda.info/vivekananda/volume_5/conversations_and_dialogues/vi_x_shri_priya_nath_sinha.htm)

Spivak had lured me into her narrative gyre,
chakravyuha—to continue Binoy's bad pun
—but trapped in its whirl, *whorl*, wheel
of fire, I was yet to emerge as its master,
the *chakravartin*, Lord of the Rings.

The hermeneutical *chaka* (circle) not yet
comprehended, completed, I had not found
my way out of the deadlock. I had not found
closure, composure. I was merely *translated*,
turned into another version of crazy Binoy.

X

I loved a girl once. But she left. Not once, not twice, not thrice, but thrice three times.

I think of her always as a girl, even after she turned woman. Because there was always a girlishness to her.

Right till she was thirty. Then it ended finally.

Funnily, her mental image of herself was quite opposite of how tiny she was.

She always thought of herself as immense, huge, size XXL, demanding king size beds and double comforters, lounging at home in enormous t-shirts dropping below her knees, underneath which she was naked.

She dreamt of big homes, big cars, big business class seats on transcontinental jetliners.

Yet she was just a wisp of a girl. A waif. A foundling. An orphan almost.

She stood outside my cast-iron wicket gate, hesitating at the threshold. Then she thrust her hand in, unlocking the latch on the inside.

It would sound with a distinct metallic click, as clear as a bell. I always recognised her arrival by the sound the latch made when she undid it.

She walked down the mossy brick path that bisected my garden, traipsing up to the large, red front door.

Again, she paused before ringing the bell.

By then I was already at the door. I had heard her and was myself waiting for her.

As I did every evening at 8:00.

Yet, she hesitated even when she knew I was on the other

side of the door, expecting her.

She knew that she would not be turned away.

But she paused awhile before she rang the bell and I opened the door. She wanted to ensure that all was well, the energy was right.

I too waited on the other side. To welcome her. With open arms.

My greeting always seemed to fill her with surprised gratitude.

Afraid of the off-chance that she would not be let in, she had that slightly anxious, questioning look, then the relief, bordering on wonder, when I scooped her up into my arms.

All this defined her—us—so perfectly.

She wasn't one, but always wore that orphan look.

So I gave her the affirmation she so needed, commanded.

I received her each evening with lavish appreciation, feeding her, listening to her chatter, her stories, her analysis, her songs, her whinges....

Then making mad, intense love to her.

Afterwards, we washed together, nuzzled in embrace, watching ourselves in the mirror.

We walked about nude, sometimes padding across to the kitchen, for dessert or coffee.

Then she left, for she could not stay the night.

Not just for that night. But even for a single night.

Night after night, she trudged back to her digs, which she shared with two others. There she woke up alone, long after her roomies left.

And I bestirred myself alone too. Exhausted. In my big empty bed in my big house.

But that was our way. That half-defiant, half-denied, dangerous liaison, sometimes flagrant in the moonlight, or disguised under cover of darkness.

Those late, late, nights defined me, defeated me, those half-licit pleasures, clandestine encounters.

Every evening I adopted her. Every night, going back alone to her bedsitter, she orphaned herself again.

There was something sad about those partings but, somehow, they also defined the happiest days of our lives.

Yet what she demanded and received did not absorb or contain her completely. It also, unfortunately, exasperated and enraged her.

One part of her was offended, another supremely gratified.

It showed in the way she walked home, night after night, with a swag. Her gnawing ache in both belly and womb placated.

And heart overflowing, brimming as if tipsy.

She had the sway of the inebriate.

Yet it incensed her, this unacknowledged, secret rendezvous. She wanted to possess me. She wanted to own this house.

But she felt intimidated by both. Except the living room and the bedroom, it seemed to shut her out.

She imagined spright-like presences of former lovers and girlfriends. Of an ex-wife too.

They bothered and frightened her, she said.

The house resisted her.

Even to smoke, she had to step out, into the garden, or climb a flight of stairs to the terrace.

There were too many rules: no meat was cooked here, no alcoholic drinks stocked or served.

Almost in retaliation, she pooped by turn in each of the four toilets, even in the one usually reserved for me, which no one else used.

Was she marking her territory?

She showered in a different loo each day, upstairs or downstairs, depending on her whim.

She used my towel, which I didn't like, disdaining the fresh one kept for her.

She also shagged off on the mattress in the puja room, delicately, with all her clothes on, but right in front of all the mounted photos of the Gods and Gurus.

"As if they care a shit," she remarked casually, "I am sure they have a damn good time, whenever they can."

Turning to me, she added, "I must cum on my own when you are not interested in me. I must look to satisfying myself howsoever

I can."

A stab at me, but false accusation? Given the frenzied bouts of nightly sex, with seldom a dry day in between?

But to accuse and berate—that became her style.

A day or two would thus pass because of her fights and sulks.

So much withholding on her part, acting oh so pricy—before giving in, coming back.

XI

A couple of years passed.

Marked by a desultory, commuting relationship, conducted from different parts of the world.

Then suddenly she dumped me.

At first, she said she only needed a time-out.

Then it became a break.

But within a fortnight, she wanted to get back together.

Needy and bleeding, I asked, "Really?!"

"Well," she replied, "yes, though not fully."

Whatever did that mean?

When I called, she pushed back, "If I need to talk to you, I'll send you an email."

She didn't take my call on Valentine's Day. She said it was meant to defraud lovers.

No wonder. That night she was out with another man.

Some days later, when I called from another country, she said, "I'm watching Modern Family. *Call me some other time."*

On weekends, she went out, drank, danced, smoked, and kissed strangers.

Then slept with two men in quick succession. One gave her shelter. Another was a lover long past.

She called me up on the very morning she went to visit the latter: "Don't hang up, I know I've been very mean to you. But I have none else to turn to."

What that meant is I was to call her back. Because she had no money in her sim card.

I didn't want to talk to her.

I was busy, in an international conference scheduled to open in an hour and a half.

"In my moments of deepest vulnerability, I still turn to you." She was crying. "Don't hang up, please don't hang up."

All the way from a cold, cold country far, far away. Without money, with no balance on her phone.

I called her back.

I thought we were getting back together. Immediately, I bought an international phone pack to talk to her. To sort things out.

I never got to use it.

That evening she slept with someone else, avoided talking to me for days.

I had to piece together the sequence of events later, matching dates with phone calls, messages, emails, and other scraps of evidence.

Only because I needed to know the truth. That was the only way to get myself out of the mess.

Then, it all felt so pointless. What good could come out of patching up with her? Or finding out the truth. Or getting rid of her?

There was unfinished business between us.

She was bad news; getting her back into my life would be the sheerest folly.

I told her so.

"I don't want us to end like this," she pleaded, "I'll send you a ticket. Please come to see me once. Just one last time."

Of course, she had no money. I bought the ticket to see her. Hers too to see me from wherever she was.

"I have a simple philosophy," she explained when she heard I had fallen, yet again, for her bait.

"There's no harm in offering what you don't have in the first place."

I should have taken the hint. I was on the point of ceasing to care. But, having committed myself to a course of action, I thought I should go through with it. Not half-heartedly, but thoroughly.

I booked rooms for us. When I arrived, however, I felt a horrible foreboding. I realised I didn't really want to see her after all.

But she would not brook refusal or stalling.

She just showed up, without letting me know her plans.

She called from downstairs.

"I am in the lobby.

I will come up and knock on your door. If you don't let me in, I'll go wait out in the cold till you let me in."

Sob. Sniffle.

I said nothing.

"If you don't respond, I'll leave quietly on the next train."

Another sob.

"I promise I won't create a scene."

I waited for a while. When I looked down from my window, I saw her outside, in the garden.

She was smoking. She looked a sight. Her mascara was running. She was in boots that came up to her knees. Sheer net stockings showed her thighs and low cut skirt, topped with a red, shiny jacket.

Stylish, but in a grubby sort of way. Her hair was a mess too, as if she'd travelled on an overnight bus. She looked hungry.

I relented, went down to the reception to see her.

"Sorry," she smiled wryly. "I need a hot shower. Care to join?"

We hadn't met in months. And she had been all over the place.

What did she look like?

Seeing my expression, she laughed, "Whaat?! You'd better behave. If you say I look like a slut I'll chew you alive."

Upstairs, she tried to have that "chat" to put things into perspective.

I said, "Go have a shower first, then some breakfast."

A hard, tired look came on her face, "Oh, so you want me to clean up and look decent? And then feed me?"

She got up. Then, turning back, half undressed, she said, "I loved you, I still love you. But I am tired of a long-distance relationship."

She walked back to kiss me. She smelled of stale cigarette smoke. Putting my hand on her breast, she smiled, "I don't want to have a Skype boyfriend."

I said, "Okay."

Half-relieved at what seemed like the end.

But from inside the bathroom, water running, she yelled, "Let's be together for a while till we can figure it out."

After she came out, wrapped in the white towel, she looked so much nicer. I gave her a hug.

"We have too much between us. We must give this a try," she said half to herself.

She looked thoughtful, as if mulling things through with quiet seriousness.

Her touch seemed vaguely familiar.

Yet strange.

Still redolent with subtle memories of what had been.

"Really?" I asked.

"Of course."

Again, she professed undying love.

"Look, I will always love you. You know that," she cried, jumping onto the bed.

The towel had dropped.

She looked a bit pinched, skinnier than ever, but the breasts were very full and firm. She knew I was looking at her. For the first time, she smiled.

"Haven't you been eating...?" I ventured.

"Only drinking," she laughed. "Strictly liquid diet."

Then, reaching for her bag, she exclaimed, "Surprise!"

She opened her purse, took out a small box.

Rings!

"I bought them from a pawnshop," she said as a matter of fact.

She put them on, pledging to be with me forever: "With this ring, I take thee..."

She had the lines by heart.

The rings were quite nice, though fake. We took pictures trying them on. They fit perfectly, hers and mine.

I said, "Are you serious? Do you want to go to Selfridges?"

She looked mock-scared, "No, no, no!"

Then laughed, "I want a big rock, not enough in your wallet for that right now, eh?"

That evening, again we fell out. She wanted me to take her shopping. She needed all kinds of stuff. Girly things too: "We'll go to something cheap and chirpy. For now. Primark?"

At Oxford Circus, she said, "I have something to confess. I haven't been a good girl."

Right in the middle of the street, she spilled the beans. Almost boasting about her indiscretions.

Men. Are so easy!

What is it about a woman offering herself that made it impossible to refuse?

She was offended when I did not react.

"You don't even care! How I have suffered. Doing this to myself.... And you don't even respond! What kind of a man are you?"

She shook me.

"Go on! Slap me. Now. Or push me under the bus if you think I've wronged you. Wuss!"

Then she started crying. "Don't hate me. Please."

Speechless, I started walking away. My head was spinning.

She followed me and screamed, "You can't walk away from me. Do you hear? I am breaking up with you. Right now!"

There, in the middle of Oxford Street, she broke up with me. Yet another time.

I waited on the footpath, heart pounding, but calm, as she ran through the traffic, away from me.

I didn't move. I had been through too much drama with her already.

She'd walked across to a pub towards Tottenham Court Road. Slowly, she turned, checked that I was still there, sitting on the pavement.

Satisfied, she beckoned to me, smiling brightly, and hollered, "Come through!"

As if nothing had happened.

The pedestrian crossing light had turned green.

I don't know why, but I followed her to the other side. I suppose I was curious. The plot was too interesting to resist.

As the evening lengthened, she drank herself to distress. "Watch out, mate," whispered the bartender replenishing her decanter, as she snuck into the Ladies.

When she emerged, her make-up was runny, as was her nose.

But she was composed. She said, calmly, that she'd gone inside to have "A little cry—and throw up."

"I wish you were there to hold my hair up," she said, with a half-smile.

Then she went out to get some fresh air and have a smoke.

But when she was back, she started drinking again.
"Why?" I asked, "Why are you doing all this?"
"To let go of you, bit by bit," she said, sobbing.
"I can't seem to give you up, though, can I?" she snorted, bitterly.
Late past midnight, she careened out of the pub. I followed, lost in my frosty breath. With each puff, her cigarette fiercely glowed.

We lost our way. None of the strangers in the night seemed
knew their London either. The city was full of foreigners,
tourists like us. Her phone was dead; no balance. Mine, with a
foreign service provider, dysfunctional. No GPS. It was cold.
I knew we were very near our hotel.
I knew this part of town from previous visits.
Yet, shrouded in the foggy darkness, we wandered about in circles.
All that walking seemed to sober her up.
We found our way back when the night was half over.

In the shower, naked, her mascara marking dark lines on her face, she began to sing.
As the water laved over her hair and body, she leaned back against the shower stall.
She could barely stand. Her breasts glistened, nipples hardened.
She knew I was looking at her, crying inside.
She began to hum, then broke into song:

তবু মনে রেখো যদি দূরে যাই চলে।
যদি পুরাতন প্রেম ঢাকা পড়ে যায় নবপ্রেমজালে।
যদি থাকি কাছাকাছি,
দেখিতে না পাও ছায়ার মতন আছি না আছি...

Remember me still, even if I go far away.
If old love gets buried under a newer ardour.
Even if I'm living nearby
you will see me not, for I'll be like the shadows.
But remember me still
If tears come to your eyes...

Half to herself, half to me she sang.
Holding both her palms out, as if asking
for alms or absolution. Letting the water
pour through them as a libation. She wept.
I was standing right in front, naked too,
in the shower. But I had lost her.

We lay in bed. She began to talk. She wanted me,
but she couldn't keep me. That was the trouble,
she explained. When the day broke, she picked
a fight again. We quarrelled, she slapped me hard, over some non-issue.
And walked out. Yet again.
The door slammed. I heard her
storming down the wooden stairs. Then all was
quiet. Was she downstairs? In the reception?
Or in the garden? Or was she actually gone?

Oh, but she left her phone behind. I saw that
and couldn't help laughing. Such a con she was.
Soon she was back, calling
from the reception, apologetic,
asking if she could come up upstairs

just to get her phone.
She returned, stayed. Now it was time for make-up sex.

As I peeled a condom, slid it on, she suddenly said,
"Wait. Let's make a baby."
"What?"
I looked at her alarmed. "Are you serious?"

"Right now, right away" she said insistently.
"Let's make this real. This is the only way."
I said nothing but didn't take the condom off.

When we were done, the sun was up.
It'd been a night of such turbulence.

But now I felt calmer. Perhaps, the day would be
different after all. Perhaps, we would live happily
ever after.
We went down to breakfast.
I wanted to check out, but she whispered,
"Let's go back up. I want you in my mouth."

"I can't let you go just like that," she said,
when we were back in our room. I stood still
as she expertly unzipped me, drawing me out.

But it felt strange. As if I didn't know her at all,
though locked in this curious intimate ritual.

For the first time in all our time together,
right in the middle of act, she gagged, rushed out
of the bedroom. I went after to check on her.

She'd doubled over the kitchen counter, puking
into the steel sink, disgorging the remnants
of the meal, stale beer—and us. Bits of our
undigested relationship spewed out.
An ugly mess, in stale, broken, stinky scraps.

I was not finished, but had to catch a flight
from the London City Airport. She fought me
all the way to Waterloo. Grabbing at my backpack
she made as if to open my laptop. "Let's see
how many times you've cheated on me!"
"You're crazy," I said, as I got out of train.

She followed me, smiling in a sneaky, furtive
way. I didn't look back. I knew I'd lost her
as I ascended the escalator. The crowds
had swallowed her up. I was alone again.

I thought this time it was truly over.

But, no, it did not end there. She didn't
give up. We saw each other again—
Norwich, Delhi, Kolkata. She said
we should go on a trip, get away from
it all.
Again the fights, the promises,
the agony, the ecstasy, the outages
the whimpering—and when I wanted
some time to be by myself, how she
at first was so supportive and all that,
then clinging, resentful, afraid she'd
lose me. She said she could not forget,
would not forgive how I'd mistreated her

Who'd mistreated whom, I asked? She was outrageous.
She was cruel. She was flamboyant in her rage,
inconsolable in her grief. She went back to her city.

She fell ill. She missed her period. I'd always used
protection, but felt very scared for a while. The last
thing I wanted was to be the father of her child.

She cackled, "Don't worry. My reproductive
system's packed up. I haven't bled for months."
Please do a test, I pleaded. "I wish I were
preggers, but I'm not!" She sounded angry.

Then she disappeared for weeks.
"I had a nervous breakdown," she claimed,
"and was hospitalised even. Where were you?"
There was no point saying I didn't even know.

She broke up again. From saying she wanted
to spend every minute of her life with me,
she flipped to a complete denial of our relationship
—"There is no us. Never was. Get lost."

She dismembered, disfigured everything,
mixed fact with fiction, invented stories,
mangled facts, conceived new fictions, alibis:
"You were my sugar daddy," nothing else.

I did not blame her. The other narrative,
I don't even want to call it the real one,
was the one she had failed at. It would
have been too painful to live with or by it.

She had the right to her version, I to mine.
She left it to me to tell my side of story.
Perhaps, hers too.
But was I up to it?
I felt stranded, trapped.

I was cornered. Distraugt. I needed help.

XII

She had wounded him and, as he lay bleeding,
locked up the clotter. She had hidden the curative
tinctured swab in some crevice, as if deep inside
her own body, spiriting it away beyond reach.
There could be no release. No reconciliation.
No revenge even. Because both implied return.

Here there was no chance of that. No "return
to sender option." The package, once delivered,
could not be sent back. There it would remain,
on the mantelpiece, waiting to be opened. Accusing.
Relentless. Radioactive. Demanding to be undone,
untied, attended to, its evil contents disgorged.

He had once suggested that all that she so resented
as his lover she would more easily accept as
his "mother." He thought his explanation was good
but her response was an even greater revelation:
"I can't mother you. When what I want is for you to be
my mother."

Her *mother*? The mother she *never*
had? He replied, nonplussed, "But how is that possible?
Well, yes, I can play your *father*, if you wish...
but your mother...?" He trailed off uncertainly.
"No, silly. I have a father. He's very sweet. I don't
have *daddy* issues. I have *mommy* problems. *Huge* ones.

So was *that* identity's last secret?
Trauma inflicted by a mother who,
worse than a stepmother, is really
a bitch? Is that what she sought
in every failed relationship, a *mother*
not a partner, lover, man, or husband?

She might have, had she wanted it,
been a mother herself. Even mother
of his child. Instead, all she craved
was for someone else to be her mother.
What any man could give her
wasn't just *good* enough.

As to fathers, she had a father already,
who suited her despite his passivity
or inability to protect her from her mother.
But his love, with its taint of sorrow,
had the touch of defeat if not loss.
It made her protective of him.

He brought out her motherly instinct;
she shielded her father from her mother.
They were secret sharers, co-victims.
That's why she didn't want a father,
only a mother. Her own mother, witch
in the grim folk tale, she hated so much.

When I met the monster, I thought, sadly,
the mother herself was a child. Especially,
in her unconcern for others, habitual
self-absorption. Her very ineptitude forced
others to take care of her. Besides, she was
the dominant bread-earner.

Both mother
and daughter were damaged, mutually injurious.
Who would care for whom? Both desperately,
so badly needy. It was a mother she wanted,
a mother she looked for in her lovers. When they
couldn't be that to her, she turned on them,

like an angry spectre, avenging angel.
To his cry, *phire esho,* she had turned.
Not toward, but away from, *against* him.
From lover, she became not his mother,
but *death-eater.* She did to him
what her mother had to her.

She turned into her own monster-mother.
Her rages were meant to conceal
what was missing in her.
A vital part, damaged or beyond repair.
He had not only become Binoy, but destined
for a fate equally bad, he too was cracking up.

[32] In Homer, Paeon, the physician of the gods, heals both Ares, god of courage and war, and Hades, god of death and the underworld.

XIII

the crazy poet's wail,
the forsaken lover's howl

(justified by jilting)
began when he and she

were over, done with, finished.
now only words, wounds, remained.

with their broken, jagged edges.
to fashion or fasten,

from screams of pain
a healing paean.[32]

only a song,
a cry, can soothe

mend, bend, blend,
or embalm a heart

broken up, broken into two,
two halves that once fit so irregularly,

now separated as messily.
where was the hymn,

tantra to restore,
reunite them?

right now,
all that remained

in that desolate landscape
of loss was separation, devastation.

the absurdity of having
and being unable to hold

the conditional bliss
that slips away

spilling so easily,
just wasted sperm,

dissolute, desolate, destitute.
how to translate such dissipation

into meaningful utterances,
sentences replete with sound and sense?

instead, what transpires
is an unintended outcome

of the parting of ways,
a tremendous blood-letting

as it were
of sheer insensibility, inconsideration—

picaresque
turning to *burlesque*.[33]

the travesty of one splitting into two,
lurching away—

raggedly tramps,
each reeling under the blow,

wending his and her own separate ways.
so merry, merrily,

very verily
bherry bherrily

kshanik-kshanik
schizophrenic

with hardly a hey nonny-nonny,
dingle-dangle, jingle jangle,

no brouhaha, *shor-sharaba*
or *khoon-kharaba:*

he was through
shillying-shallying,

groaning, moaning
keening-preening

[33] "Nobody really knows where the word burlesque came from—some claim its roots are the Italian and Spanish words '*burla*,' which mean 'hoax' and 'deception' respectively." *Burla* has also been translated as 'jest.' Burlesque was invented in Victorian England, perhaps as a need of the times. Its forte was that it satirised highbrow opera, ballet, and costume drama, which were unavailable to the masses. It was, quintessentially, a musical variety show, both entertaining and funny. When it crossed the Atlantic to the United States, burlesque added the added attraction of semi-clad female dancers. "Soon, these sexually suggestive routines became the focus of the performances, and the word burlesque became a synonym for striptease...." (http://www.pulpinternational.com/pulp/keyword/Tempest+Storm.html)

For decades, Indian popular cinema had the mandatory "cabaret," whose origins are in burlesque. Even today, the form persists in the item song. Earlier performed by specialists called "vamps," now, increasingly, heroines and stars themselves enact it.

whether in groin
or loin.

no noble art,
the moral of this art

was more like a smelly fart,
from its very start.

she was no queen of hearts,
but a slimy, slinky tart.

what!—*auchitya-bhango?*
violation of decorum?

dun' care,
dun' matter—

de-co-rum?
more like *dick-cum-rump*.

artistic impropriety?
more likely *pimp-prick-titty*

auchitya-bhango
or *o-chutiya-bung'ole?*

this end-note
end-nut?

(pronounced end-*not*
or end-*knot*)

connotes,
con(t)-notes
cont-nuts

whatever you may

fatuously construe
fartuosly con(t)-crew...

kindly continue
sorry, cont help it,

contly continue
the seventh stage of love,

one that follows *junoon*
or frenzied obsession,

is not *fana,*
sublimation of all passion,

but *chutiyapa*
(screwed over or buggered)

as the one-and-a-half dick-shits
(*dedh ishqiya*),

swear to their equally
contemptible,

contemporary,
counterparts

cont-c-farts[34]
culinary arts

[34] *Dedh Ishqiya* (2014), dir. Abhishek Chaubey: "*Ishq ke saat mukaam hote hain—dilkash, uns, mohabbat, akeedat, ibaadat, junoon aur fanaa....*" But, as Khaalu Jaan (Naseeruddin Shah) declares, the seventh is actually *chutiyapa*, something utterly worthless or futile.

therefore,
memsucker of mayhem

from Murshidabad or Mymensingh,
mis*lay* no more men

with your
crazy c✿ntundrums

c✿nt-tantrums,
(connundrums)

panties and aunties
panjandrums

of must-must (*mast-mast*)
madness.

cease, desist or re-join
your myriad minions,

lugubrious
legions,

mashis & *pishis*
mournful cousins

(*mish-mash,*
pish-pash)

squadrons of scullions
gnashing their teeth,

a union of moaners,
willing wailers,

crooning in slow motion,
singing in unison,

baying to the moon like banshees,
heads up-tilted...

O miss muppet
from Phuket

(*fuckit?*)
with delicious breasts,

how very pretty,
your pointy little titties...

da titties—
singing ditties

missy-lizzie
dolefully, desolate

shitties
(pronounced *she-eats*)

of melodious
hits

(pronounced *he-eats*)
all-time favourites

(pronounced *phev-reats*)
of *Robindroshongeet—*

what else would you expect?
(*gheat eat?*)

Bitch of Norwich
beach of *no-reach*

retch and roll over,
eat crow,

wicked witch
(*wheach*)

lick-no-dick,
(*dhak-dhak dheak)*

smutty butty,
(*smitten-beauty*),

snooty-snotty
nastie-bestie

quietly expire
or burst into instant flames,

burning brightly
internally combust,

(*cum bust*)
kumbukht

c❀n(t)-bus(t)
suct-n-muct,

incinerate,
disintegrate—

swat your twat
hoe your hoo-ha,

on your ownsome
lonesome,

(loan some
loathsome)

whilst i sing ha-ha,
la-la,

na-na,
are baba—ta-ta

and i,
once so *seedha-saadha,*

now shoddy-shitty,
sodden silly

pricky-potty,
feckless-fecker,

willy-nilly
whoratio-fellatio,

phoota-phoda,
bring this coda

—post-frigged,
post-script,

scrotum, scriptum,
squirtum,

cum, cum,
yum, yum

slit from the crypt
sliding down shit creek,

to a swift
and certain

khatam,
(c❀nt-um, come on)

kandam-condom,
condemn-cartoon

tun tun, tum tum
to an end.

but beware,
may none take offence

at my *tu-tu, mai-mai*
thu-thu

or they'll get one more blinking blister
on their blasted

butty-smutty,
booty-potty.

so, enough!
avaunt, (s)cumbag!

take your leave,
al vida,

from
kutia-chutia,

whose-dearest-blessed-breastie
was your erstwhile nastie nestie.

now quit her sight!
chut-chute,

so cute
vanish like a fart, go—

dreadful minister of smell
to your own private hell.

ada pada kon pada
damaji ka ghoda pada

taan-tuun, taam-tuum, dhaam-dhuum,
kuchka brahman pada tu.

arty-smarty, who's the farty?
damaji's dungy horse's fatty

tann-tuun, taam-tuum, dhaam-dhuum,
O rotten brahmin it's you who's let loose.[35]

so this is the way the tempest ends
of the beauty and the beast

(booty and bust)
after the plot has thickened and stiffened

not with a bang or whimper,
but in a farty fierce farce.

[35] Like "Eeny, meeny, miny, moe," this is a children's selecting rhyme to discover who farted, whether loudly or malodourously.

Thus
i went mad.

but being unhinged
was only a temporary diversion,

no solution.
the recognition, detection, uncovering of character and motive,

the heart of any narrative still eluded me.
but *was* i close!

i did not possess the vital bit that could pry open the crack,
(though i could smell it).

i knew i couldn't fall apart like this,
not without figuring, *frigging,* out the truth.

a real woman had driven me insane.
trying to make a fictional character

out of her would not bring her back.
this much i discerned.

but could it restore
my sanity?

could writing do that?
Twat? i asked myself,

as the bitch-witch,
who had me so *bewitched,*

disappeared
into the mist in Norwich.

XIV

He was left alone in the grand cathedral,
which they'd started erecting
a thousand years ago
in the old kingdom of East Anglia.
Most of it was merely flint and mortar,
but topped with a lovely, creamy limestone.
Slabs of stone were mined near Caen,

a town across the border, in today's France.
Lithic quarries formed 167 million years ago,
in Jurassic times, yielded the dolomite in shallow
lagoons. It was easy to mine. The cathedral
was begun after the Norman conquest of 1066,
in times when England and France were one
nation. The grand edifice they conceived

was dedicated to the Holy and Undivided Trinity.
Suddenly, he became aware that there was
beside him and her, always a third.
Man and woman are not alone,
separately set, left to fend for themselves
in a fallen world. What unites them,
in Christian terms, is the holy spirit.

Or, as Yajnavalkya said to Maitreyi,
"It is not for the sake of the husband
that the wife loves the husband, but
for the sake of the Self." It is only
in that sacredness do they come together,
two-becoming-one, sanctified, blessed.

Else, a mere coupling of two bodies
is always bound to fail or fall apart.
She may have gone, but he was not alone
Or abandoned. Because God as Guru walked
with him, though invisible. Now within,
he felt the holy presence. T. S. Eliot knew this.
"Who is the third," he asked, "who walks

always beside you? When I count,
there are only you and I together.
But when I look ahead up the white road
There is always another one walking beside you
Gliding wrapt in a brown mantle, hooded...."
From the *Wasteland* the lines resurfaced
so expectedly. Eliot too had found

a guiding light in Julian of Norwich.
He had quoted her, earliest of English
women writers, in *Little Gidding*. Now inside
the same, grand, glorious cathedral, he saw
the statue of the mystic-anchorite, known simply
as Julian, in *Revelations of Divine Love*
(circa 1373 CE) says: "Sin is Behovely, but

All shall be well, and all manner of thing
shall be well." He was well. All had
to be well. The fog in his brain cleared.
All he could do was to cry.
She had left him to tell a story. That was all
he had to go by, to save himself.
Everything else was wrecked, broken.

She had pushed him away and now
he too knew what it was like
to be outside, always in the cold,
midst the raging storm. No security,
no stability, no settling down, no warm
interiors or cosy bedrooms. Indoors
scared her. Shelter was not only too good

to be true, but too bad to lose. Always,
everywhere, she recreated the storm.
That was her element. Not halcyon winds
blowing ships back ashore. Wounded,
she reconfirmed her wound. Poking it
just before it healed. It was the only thing
that truly marked her. Her need, her gash,

insatiable, incurable, her own unhealing
abrasion, laceration. It was the only way
to justify herself. Her wound defined, validated
her. Damaged, she did not, *could not,* love.
Therefore *nobody* must. If anyone tried,
she would pierce and slash him too
so horribly he'd recoil, terror-struck.

That dread disfiguring—that was her triumph.
"See, you cannot love me. Even *you* cannot.
You too have failed, as others before you."
Then came the punishment, implacable,
remorseless, unrelenting, inflict it she must.
Found unsatisfactory, she condemned him,
her latest sacrifice, to a fate similar to hers.

"I now pronounce you a failure in love.
Inadequate, useless, no good for anyone else
or the world, you are damaged goods. Only
I can accept and take care of you. You have
nowhere else to go, nowhere to turn. You are
mine, only mine now—and forever more
you shall remain in my custody and thraldom.

To do with you as I please is now my right.
Get used to it; it's an improvement over death."
She had to show that all the love in the world
was too poor, too scanty before her cavernous need.
If her unfortunate victim, maimed and marked
for sacrifice, managed to hobble away,
still able to escape—then her wound would

reopen. She would retreat into her own
private hell—another suicide attempt,
nervous breakdown, or fasting for days,
in a catatonic daze. Weeping at bus stops,
street corners, shopping malls till she attracted
another saviour, caregiver, *anyone* to take her
in, wringing out tears, oaths, imprecations,

or prayers till it actually happened. Her waif-hood
reconfirmed, it was her way to cope with a breakup,
a move she had perfected by failing at love so often.
Still the feline self-preservation remained. Her basic
instinct intact, she hid her illness so cunningly,
especially from those who mattered most.
She never broke down at work, in front of bosses

superiors, colleagues, or parents of lovers. Authority
figures who might endanger her professionally,
were never privy to her rages or ravages.
Her plunges into exaggerated grief, dramatic fits,
were for the benefit of strangers or intended victims
and caretakers. Wherever the affirming, safe embrace,
backhanded confirmation of support from a universe

not completely hostile, that had not entirely given up
on her, could be ascertained, especially when it came to
men, she would once again use her lubricious prowess
to attract and subdue them. Kindness from strangers
was safest because it was her only comfort and last
resort after throwing her own love to the wolves.
It was all she could afford when she'd squandered

all her heart's savings. But love, thus mistreated,
will seek its vengeance, always coming back to bite
its betrayer. No matter that she was ever
the drama queen, her performance a clever cover up.
Whatever she was trying to hide would always
show up. Eventually. For love too is hazardous:
Why choose love when you can be happy?

But what was she so afraid to disclose? What was
so important that it had to escape detection?
Wasn't it identity's last secret? What remained
so tenaciously hidden that it insistently cried out
the loudest? What ended up showing in every action,
surreptitiously rearing its head in each spoken word?
The more it is hidden, it hits you all the more

in your face. Her rages were meant to conceal
that missing part. Either congenital or acquired
during a bruised, damaged childhood. Her wound.
That had turned into an extreme, desperate,
im*passable*, im*possible* pass. Its very intractability
made her run and hide. Abandon those she loved
or who loved her. But before the discarding,

something else, even more defining, dreadful.
One more thing, worse, more devastating.
The mark she left on her lovers—the damaging,
disfigurement, excoriation, penalty exacted. Hidden
in her, but made visible in those she preyed upon.
Only then could the disowning be explained,
justified. What she could not possess, could not keep,

she must wreck. In the end that was most revealing,
incriminatory. Her terrible secret exposed, the plot,
ploy, turned deadly. A denouement of destruction,
monstrous mutilation. A wound, *another*
wound. Reciprocal. Perpetual. Perpetrated
by the one originally wounded.
Wounded, wounding.[36]

XV

Spivak responded to Binoy's book of poems by recounting her engagement with the protocols of the text. She did not pay attention to its "personal" elements, including his dedication, *deification,* even address of the text to her.

For Spivak, all these aspects were subsumed under the protocols of the text.

But caught out more than once, at first resisting—then yielding—to the temptations of the text, she (mis)identifies herself as the addressee of a mad poet's fantasies. Though ostensibly finding it impossible to offer any response other than a textual one, she admits to herself and to her readers, in the end, that she, indeed, is the poet's imaginary "Dream Girl."

Has she betrayed herself, the poet, or her own delineation of the protocols of the text?

Or is it Spivak's double dodge a case, so to speak, of having your fudge and eating it too?

She can claim that she has nothing to do with the addressee or the person Binoy dedicated his book to. But it is the *protocols* of the text that demand that she admit that she is the person referred to, even though in that capacity she could not, *never*, respond, let alone reciprocate.

[36] The sickness of the times, Kaliyuga, causes an inflammation not just within us, but in the whole world around us. As the Tathagata said, "Monks, everything is on fire. What is on fire? The six sense organs—eyes, ears, nose, tongue, body and mind—are all on fire. The six objects of the senses—form, sound, smell, taste, touch, and objects of mind—are all on fire. The six consciousnesses—sight, hearing, smell, taste, feeling, and thought—are all on fire. They are all burning from the flames of desire, hatred and illusion. They are burning from the flames of birth, old age, sickness, and death, and from the flames of pain, anxiety, frustration, worry, fear, and despair.

Monks, every feeling is burning whether it is unpleasant, pleasant, or neutral feeling. Feelings arise and are conditioned by the sense organs, objects of the sense organs, and the sense-consciousnesses. Feelings are burning from the flames of desire, hatred and illusion. Feelings are burning from the flames of birth, old, age, sickness, and death, and from the flames of pain, anxiety, frustration, worry, fear, and despair.

Monks, do not allow yourselves to be consumed by the flames of desire, hatred, and illusion. See the impermanent and inter-dependent nature of everything in existence in order not to be enslaved by the cycle of birth and death created by the sense organs, objects of the senses, and the sense-consciousnesses" (http://cuckooscall.blogspot.com/2006/07/fire-sutra.html). —*Ādittapariiyāya Sutta* or *Āditta Sutta*, the Buddha's third sermon, is included in the *Saḷāyatanavagga* of the Samyuttanikāya and in the Vinaya Mahāvagga.

Is that *identity's last secret?*

Yet, in her translation into English of the Bangla original, isn't she satisfying Binoy's entreaties? If so, is it as a reader, pure and simple, a *mere* reader that she renders such service to the poet?

Or is it Binoy's "Dream Girl" herself, his *Ishwari*, Goddess, who has at last answered his prayers, albeit posthumously, by taking upon herself the onus of making his work known to the world?

Is that her own indirect way of contributing to, even amplifying, Binoy's apotheosis of her?

By translating his work, is she telling the world, "See how I was worshipped by one of the most gifted poets of my generation?"

Or does she, instead, imply, "He was one of the most gifted poets of his generation, hence deserves wider recognition. As reader/critic/translator, I am doing what I can to make his work known to a wider audience.

"As to the poet's being in love with me, dedicating his book to me—well, that is purely his business. I have nothing to do with it one way or another. It is merely yet another aspect of the text, its special protocol, which I—or any reader—might take into consideration.

"My relationship with the person portrayed by Binoy is as near or distant as to any other character that he might have drawn.

"I have nothing to do with Binoy's Gayatri. That she is me is what he imagined. To me, I have as little to do with her as to any other fictional or poetic oddity."

But, we think the lady protests too much. All these ruses only afford her—and us—a partial return, textual, *transcendental,* rather than real satisfaction or closure.

XVI

Spivak's critical chronicle, tucked away
in a recessed crevice between the bounteous
shanks—a big, fat theory book, reveals
when bared, only a half-truth, like a secret organ

or private part: *recovery is possible in translation*.
But what *kind* of recovery?
Full or only partial,
that remains to be seen...

In fact, it is less than it seems.
For Spivak, paradoxically, it is a recovery
that transcendentalises love, translating it
literally from earth to heaven, from the here

to the hereafter, from reality to metatextuality.
It is, ironically, the sort of solution to love's double bind
that the entire logic of her book deplores and resists.
The robust call to de-transcendentalise, repeated

almost like a chant, a mantra,
fails to live up to its promise. Or,
even more cleverly, it was never
meant to. It is only a ploy, play, ultimate

sleight of hand, to mislead and evade.
De-transcendentalisation is nothing more
than distracted theory. Actually, Spivak
succumbs to the unlikely seductions

of mysticism by another name
or garb, albeit under the cover
of cultural materialism. After all,
political correctness trumps both

reason and common sense, making
monkeys or braying asses of men.
We say and do things utterly contrary
to what we profess. "De-transcendentalise"

is itself a mask for another form
of transcendentalism: the Brahmin
girl, so to say, can give up Brahminism,
but Brahminism will not give up Gayatri.

Like Derrida, one of Spivak's acknowledged gurus,
or Marx, whom she has taught each term for forty years,
both of who are really Jewish prophets in disguise.
Like Marx, *for Marx*, Derrida offered not criticism,

but theology. The prophecy of redemption through
radical deconstruction. Freedom wrought through
another version of textual paradox or unravelling?
How everything at once means itself—

and also its exact opposite *at the same time*.
Thereby the two cancel each other. Such is
the Derridean *via negativa*, deconstruction,
freedom from "thingness." Every*thing*

thus, ingeniously, is shown as *no-thing*.
Impermanence, absence, emptiness,
instead of metaphysics of presence.
Anti-essence. Seeing this—seeing *thus*,

unlike the fissure of the atom, does not release
liberating energies, catapulting us out
of the clutches and bondage of identity
and signification. Such release, alas, is just

and always a kind of game, a word-game even,
the release generated, too, realisable
only in the intersections, *interstices,* of textuality—
a dissatisfying, *dizzying,* disincarnate kind of freedom.

Inducing an unbearable longing, dire anticipation,
of prophets awaiting promised messiahs.
Such prophecies also breed false expectations
in an endless series of postponements.

As V.S. Naipaul knew only too well,
it is not so much the belief
in the existence of justice that is
at the "root of so much human anguish,"

but the delusion of *expectation* itself.[37]
Nothing corrodes the human spirit
as much as expectation, nothing
leads to as much anguish. To be

beguiled first and belied at last—
that is the very nature of expectation.
Similarly, the pleasures of deferral
are confined, after all, by its very nature:

what is promised and much-awaited,
must by its very logic, also be deferred.
So also the redemption such as
deconstruction offers is deferred.

[37] V.S. Naipaul, *Literary Occasions* (New York: Vintage, 2004): "I had arrived at the conviction—the conviction that is at the root of so much human anguish and passion, and corrupts so many lives—that there was justice in the world."

XVII

Endlessly, deferred.
Spivak's solution to the problem of the double bind,
must remain similarly playful,
rather than prayerful or powerful.

It is only in the recreation, *re-creation,* of words
that the escape from the double bind is offered.
But the double bind, too, is merely textual in the first place.
Only apparently real, crushing, or deadly.

Apparently real, but actually textual—
such as also the release it offers.
Only Spivak, the conjurer, sorceress, high priestess
of linguistic twists and turns

can show us the secret trap door out of her double bind.
Trap door:
door that releases even as it traps.
Similarly,

translation:
which *recovers*
even as it *betrays*
the "original."

Her adoring poet dead, his unrequited love is translated into poetry.
He himself is dead,
translated by his own reckoning from earthly sorrows
to heavenly joys.

Only in heaven, then, as projected from earthly miseries,
is the paradise imagined in poetry.
There, it still awaits conjugal felicity,
as in a parallel universe,

imagined only by the poet.
Offered as consolation to the reader,
Binoy suffers
in silent solitude

as if in his private purgatory
—or heaven
of his own making.
There Gayatri, his dream-girl

Goddess
Divine Paramour
Iswari
translated

after her own rendition of Binoy's Bangla,
is to unite with him,
both of them youthful, still embodied,
in flesh (re)incarnate.

Gayatri: the girlfriend Binoy would have had,
but couldn't in 1961.
Chaka,
the wheel that wouldn't turn back

now translated into his "Dream Girl"
if only in the poems,
apotheosised later into his *Iswari*
—Goddess—

finally his eternal spouse in heaven
where he still awaits her arrival though
on earth till the very end of his demented days,
Gayatri staunchly and studiously ignored him.

How to do justice to such passion, such loss?
What recompense for the mad poet and his unrequited love?
Only translation?
But even that as yet only a promise,

a prophecy for the future,
its fulfilment postponed for now and forever?
Spivak, yclept Gayatri,
after the secret mantra,

revealed to that most ambitious of the ancient rishis,
Viswamitra, the friend of the universe,
who discovered the secret bridge to the undying realms of Brahman.

Reaching the highest estate of Brahmarishi,
vaulting over every barrier.
Gayatri: the mantra,
when mastered,

translates us from mere mortality to immortality,
in bodies armoured with light
Gayatri—
tat savitur varenyam....

Gayatri,
the mantra that epitomises translation.
Gayatri,
the translator translated.

Gayatri,
de-transcendentaliser,
Gayatri,
herself transcendentalised.

Gayatri,
knowing all this,
Gayatri,
yet failing to do.

XVIII

Now his soul, hyena-like, howls its anguish.
No, no, way out. Another dead end,
stream run aground, dried up. His release,
resolution must lie elsewhere. Not here
with Spivak or her double-b(l)ind, false
promises of recovery, leading only to

translation. Even if his love is dead,
he needs something else, something more.
In the meanwhile, the wound still bleeds,
in quiet suppuration, if not blazing,
blinding pain. Yet it leaves a track,
trail, of blood. It could lead him on.

It is Jeanette Winterson, not Spivak,
who throws a rope to the drowning sailor,
cast overboard. Even as he sputters, suffocates,
out of breath, he finds a way to untie the knot
of deconstruction, de-transcendatalisation,
that will release him from the double-bind.

He knows he needs a new literary form,
a new bridge, a new textual artifice,
like a new incantation or mantra, what
Sri Aurobindo called *The Future Poetry,*
idiom of the impossible and miraculous,
the special net of words to snare the catch.

Not to bring back or recapture the lost love.
But to be able to love again. Not the object
of love matters, but the ability to love.
Meditation is not; getting used to is.[38] Poetry
cannot be turned into a plea, but it is prayer.
Come back, come back—the crazy Orphic howl

of Dionysius for Persephone, or his scouring
the underworld, is not merely a cry of distress, not
just an appeal. Not just, *come back*, *come back*,
or don't leave, don't end this, don't let us cease
upon the midnight with so much pain, not just
phire esho chaka. Instead, it is to find

one's way back to oneself, not to one's dream girl.
The *chaka* (or Chakravorty) would not return.
That was fantasy, delusion, lofty expectation,
thus destined to be belied, shattered. It could
only lead to dissatisfactions of private anguish
or public declarations of inconsolable loss

in verse or worse. As Binoy knew: "I will now
be mad, at last by insane claws/ Will prise out
the angel's home address, the door." But
the angel's address could not be found,
her door could not prised open. The poet
knew only madness—and death—both

[38] Sogyal Rinpoche, *The Tibetan Book of the Living and Dying* (New York, HarperCollins, 2003): "There is a revealing Tibetan saying, '*Gompa ma yin, kompa yin*,' which means literally: 'Meditation' is not; 'getting used to' is. It means that meditation is nothing other than getting used to the practice, of meditation."

romantic in poets, especially in our sub-continent
of sentiment. Instead of waiting for her return,
Binoy ought to have let her go. Rather than
expecting her, at some future date, to piece together
the torn bits of a letter without an address, gone astray
—which is how he saw himself—he should have

like Winterson, used his wound to lead him back
if not to his *hriday-wsvari*, his heart-Goddess, then
to the source of pain, separation, parting, heartbreak.
Winterson to Winterson, errant-author-daughter
to irate-monster-mother, red telephone booth
to red telephone booth, even if the *pip pip pip*s

meant more and more coins, *baje khoroch,*
wasteful expenditure of both purse and heart—
as Jeanette, knew very well—were well worth
the try. Jeanette followed the blood trail that led
back to her demented mother. She healed herself if not
the delinquent mother. It was a trail, *trial,* of words,

but redder and more crimson than blood. Brooding,
pondering, waiting patiently, seeking to find
the source of the wound, the wounded finding
at last the wounder. Oh, the *wonder*! Binoy
should have used his blood trail to bring him
to his "Dream Girl." To make her real rather

than transcendental, *translated*. The whole point
being to make words count. The real person must
cease to be a character. Not the other way round.
Flesh is only too fragile. It must become word.
And word made world, the poet conjures her back,
anew. That is the logic of de-transcendentalisation,

the imperative of the rewor(l)ding what has been
deconstructed, deterritorialised. The transformation
that turns the never-healing wound into remedial
libation, not disabling violation. The double bind turns
into a twin release, the found-lost becomes
the lost-found, translated back into the original.

That was the way to emerge out of the vortex
of the *chakravyuha,* as *Chakravarty,* conqueror,
rather than victim. By learning the secret
of the wound from Winterson, he realised
that he must write his way out of the double bind.
Not back to the one he loved, but back to the truth.

More glorious, more palpable, real—instead
of waiting for her to come back, to turn, to return.
Binoy's was the tried and tested way to failure,
the way of Devdas, of self-inflicted crucifixion.
It was not the way of fullness or fulfilment.
Eschewing that compulsion towards Thanatos,

he had to chase love back to her secret lair,
to her original hiding place, its wound-womb-tomb.
From fantasy to certainty. That is why
Winterson had rejected her birth-mother,
the one who wanted her back, was proud
of her, at last, even offering to love her.

Jeanette returned to mad Mrs Winterson
instead: the deranged, damaged, fanatic,
with her revolver in the drawer, copper-tipped
bullets in a separate can, who had locked her out
of the house, making her sit on the doorstep
through the night till her bum froze, even unto

the breaking light of dawn. Which revealed
her thus shut out to neighbours. But yet
Jeanette did not cave in, but struck back,
in her own way, with the fierce courage
that only children could have, drinking up
the two pints of milk delivered to the doorstep,

walking two and a half miles to school. After
the success of her first book, Jeanette went back
not to her birth-mother, but the ogress who had
adopted—and abused her—wrong baby, *wrong crib*,
she had often complained, *devil's work.*
Because, bad as she was, Mrs Winterson

was the only mother Jeanette had. You can't deny
your mother even if you hate her. Even if her only
maternal contribution was to wound her,
Jeanette would have to make peace with it.
She would have to rewrite the trauma of the wound,
learning, Chiron-like, to heal herself and others

through the misprision of imagination. The way
of words, or blood turned into verse, the only
way of writers and artists. At the end of which
exertion of writing, from and beyond the wound,
a great realisation dawns: love is, not only loss.
Why is the measure of love loss? This is how

Winterson had begun one of her books,[38]
flagging the question, flogging her anguish,
revealing her wound. But loss is not the only
measure of love. Even if it is *one* measure,
it is merely that, one, not the *only*. The wound
in its very scarring, however scary, shows up

the blister—the stigmata of the bliss that was
once love. But it is not the blister that is the sole
seed of truth. It is also love that is true; that is why
its loss wounds us so. That is why it is unbearable,
immeasurable, impossible to overcome
or compensate. That is why its humiliation

remains on our body, in raised letters, like welts,
which we must read to find our way out, *back*.
If the measure of love is loss, then the measure
of loss is also love. In love, we become shameless.
We have no wish to hide its sores or scars. Like
the pod of a rare plant, our heart bursts into thousands

of spores. We're emptied of our suffering but our love,
born out of pain can make the desert bloom, fertilising
the earth. No more doubts arise. We do not distrust stories
—or as in Binoy's case, poems. The compensatory
mechanisms of imagination are not false or beguiling.
Writing is truth, harsh at times—sometimes anaesthesia,

sometimes anodyne.
Life itself is unbearable.
We make up for its losses
by drowning our sorrow in words.
We drink deep of that cup,
as we would the waters of Lethe.

We sleep,
we forget.
We wake up,
we recover.
What we cannot
accomplish in words

[38] *Written on the Body* (1992).

sometimes happens in real life,
comes to us unasked, unbeknownst.
A blessing. An act of grace.
A word, a mantra—suddenly
turns into a woman. Words,
in poems, in stories, actually

come true in real life.
Words help it happen,
help bring into being
the miraculous rose,
reborn from a fire
immaculate. Words

not only make up for what we have lost.
Not only lead us back, but also take us beyond
loss. For the ultimate union does not
require the object, is beyond gain and loss:
sringara, the erotic mood, consists both
of *vipralambha* and *sambhoga*.

In *karuna*, unbearable pity,
even death is dissolved. Then
what of loss? The *Advaita*
of love is to be able
to accept and enjoy both
separation and union equally.

Seeing one as not the opposite,
as much as its other side, is to see
loss as a kind of love and love
as another name for loss.
It is to be able to have and to hold
the real as well as the verbal.

To combine,
unusually,
Spivak and Winterson
is to keep one's faith.
Even after
it is lost.

XIX

We want our love stories to continue after we die.
Failing in this life, Binoy wished his love an afterlife,
following such earthly misery, in the mansion of the Gods.

Jeanette too wanted her silent screams to be heard,
her true story to turn into fiction, to be retold
in a form that she could salvage from the ashes

of her burnt-out childhood. She wished at least
her story, albeit fictionalised, would survive not just
her broken past, but her own death, in the tenuous

afterlife of literary fame. This is what
identity's last secret discloses.
A love story beyond the double bind

of double endings, contrary conclusions.
So much pain shouldn't all go to waste.
Some prose, pregnant with possibilities, poised

after the parting, must also be offered. As also verse
or worse, as appropriate libation for the second coming.
Finally, the secret revealed, not as obituary or requiem

of loss, but reticent resurrection.
For all this to transpire, the wound
has to be uncovered. In the hurt is also

the cure. The enigma of the wound
was not unknown to Spivak. Yet her double bind,
however painful, wasn't really a crucifixion

or even bleeding lesion. Her ache if real, was dull.
It did not sting or scream its anguish. Textual trouble
isn't, after all, torture. It does not wrack the soul.

But writing, *writhing*, riding the bruise, so tender
to touch, inflamed and flailing, it is Winterson
who knows the secret of the wound.

He understood at last. He had to admit it:
"I am wounded. My wound, at long last, is exposed.
Defenceless, unguarded, utterly vulnerable.

Gaping wide, open, susceptible to the mischief
or wickedness of anyone who wishes to injure me."
Worse, he could, *would*, be hurt again.

He had no resistance, no guard, no shield, no cover.
Why? Not because he was sensitive, sympathetic,
delicate, but because he was dissimilar if not distincitive.

He could never be like the others—*wrong baby, wrong crib.*
His difference was his curse, his blessing. To be free,
he had to accept, not try to deny or escape the wound.

The immediate remedy to his malady was locked
inside the one who had also struck the blow.
Whatever her purpose in inflicting

such an injury, there was now no recourse
to her or return to his prior condition.
No medication, *meditation,* mediation would draw

her back. She was gone. Nor did he know or care
to find his way back to her. He was bleeding,
but that did not bother him. He must not become

slave to the wound. Anguished, felled,
knocked out, without fleeing or forgetfulness,
now he himself must not want her return.

He had lost interest in a malaise whose lips,
painted scarlet, promised a false cure, for now
he too had a wound that would never heal

like the reminder, *remainder,* of another life.
Here, at last, was the great teaching, but
how painfully he had stumbled upon it!

The lesson and secret of the wound—
the wound was still unguarded, bare.
It was a secret path, like a trail of blood.

The missing part, most private,
Yet most exposed, was the wound.
Gash, slit, cavity, dip, abyss,

or yawning void, the wound was
also an opening. Beckoner to the beyond,
it could lead back to the source.

More than secret-sacred rituals,
more than protestations and vows,
it was the wound that let to reunion.

Only the mistress or wizard of the wound
could heal both the wounder
and the wounded, both self and other.

Only s/he deserved the title *Chakravarty.*
Conqueror. Not Spivak, with her textual
tricks, *trysts.* But another Gayatri,

mantra dishabille. His wound gave him access
to her. Like another language learned, but forgotten,
written in the alphabet of pain.

Not visual, but tactile.
Like Braille.
He had to read the welts

on his flesh, the marks
where she had carved her initials,
keeping score of her victories—

his pain, her gain.
He had to rewrite the script,
find out how no longer to be

the bondsman of pain. The wound
itself knew identity's last secret.
How to heal, be whole, and holy.

Victim at first of the sorceress
of innumerable enchantments, then
long-serving apprentice,

finally he had become
master of the wound, himself
wizard and healer of heartaches.

XX

Like a shell, not on a beach,
but carried far inland, on a dried riverbed.
The river changed course a thousand years ago,
then lost itself in the desert wastes.

Still how wide its banks,
how deep the gorge it cut through rock and soil.
Now nothing more than sandy desolation,
an immense scar on the face of the earth.

Seen even in satellite images,
a wound marks a land parched for hundreds of miles.
Yet, these fossil traces,
powdery bones of creatures once pulsating with life.

Little shells bleached white,
drying in the harsh sun,
brittle and crumbling to powdery dust at the slightest touch.
Still, once in a while, a rare, almost perfect shell.

So fragile, so singular, so pure.
Pick it up and hold it to your ear—
the echo of water,
though faint and distant, not entirely lost.

There was a river here once.
It fertilised the fields, fed the land.
It flowed down to the sea.
But the river cannot turn back,
cannot return to its origins,
up in the hills.
It must flow down to the sea or run aground,
going dry, dying.

We can never return to the womb
of our birth mother whence we were
pushed out into the cruel world.
Our mother herself sometimes turns

against us, muttering *you are not mine.*
But to our cosmic mother's womb,
which birthed the stars and galaxies,
our return is secure.

Thus the empty shell
with its echo of water sings, *rain, rain.*
Perhaps it will rain.
Perhaps, the river will flow again.

To the sea it will go.
As it will, it must course.
And if there is river,
there must be the ocean.

That, like the primal waters
from which life emerged, is our home.
Like a curse.
Like a blessing.

XXI

Now is the time to invoke the ancient spell:
It does not die.
Love persists.
It revives after it is lost.
It recoups its losses.
It lives again.
Someplace else, some otherwise.
Love has not turned deaf or silent.
Even after being wounded, left for dead, it has spoken out.
It would have done so even from beyond the grave.
As a single blade of grass,
sheer in its solitude, fragile, unimportant, unnoticed,
but there—alive, a sentinel,
speaking through its muteness, *thusness,*
proclaims the fact of its resurrection,
lonely insurrection.
Love tongues its pain,
even when cut out and left bleeding,
like Philomel.
It will speak through the language of silence or pain.
Or through a mantra named Julian, Jeanette, or Gayatri.
This is how its mutilated tongue will cry out.
Love will be found again.
Because death is so uncertain
and love so contrarian.
Love refuses to die even when it is killed.
It prepares to die,
it readies itself for the fatal blow,
like a gazelle offering its neck to the hunter.
It feels the sharp, swift stroke of the blade.
It bleeds.
It haemorrhages.
Its heart is stilled, its breath ceases.
It is deeply mourned.
Even buried or cremated.
With due ceremony or unfeelingly, summarily, perfunctorily.
Then, miraculously, it discovers that it is not dead after all.
Like a character in a children's comic book.
It quietly bestirs, dusting itself.
Love gets up,
quietly, unobtrusively,
gets going. Doing
its business,
which is
only to be,
to
love.

XXII

Yes,
love survives.
It endures somehow.

It does not entirely
give up its ghost.
It refuses to submit fully to the wound.

It retains its dignity.
It bends, O so, so low.
It breaks, in so-o-o many places.

But it chooses to live.
It will not be disowned.
Flung out, it still returns.

The wound
leads back to love,
even as it leads away from it.

We, the wounded are not accursed,
while the others, unblemished,
remain in a state of grace.

The wound marks us,
but we are not marred by it.
The wound our sigil, the symbol of our difference.

It is all we have.
It is nothing to crow about,
it is no scarlet letter,

but red badge of courage.
It is how we are bound
to the Beloved.

It is our way back.
We are wounded.
We are also blessed.

There is nothing funny about what we lose
—but somewhere in between,
there hangs this poem,

like a trapeze artist,
precarious, perilous,
but still alive.

3

Tantra

Chakrasamvara and Vajravarahi, c. 1575–1600, Malla Period, Nepal

This stunning 2 ft x 2.5 ft painting, distemper on cotton, which hangs in Gallery 252 of the Metropolitan Museum, New York, depicts Chakrasamvara and Vajravarahi from the Kathmandu Valley, Nepal.[40]

The twelve-armed deity, Chakrasamvara, is depicted in a vibrant and vigorous embrace with his consort, Vajravarahi. It has been described as "a highly charged vision by an advanced master of tantric Buddhism" (ibid). The powerful dynamics of colour, with Chakrasamvara in blue, his palms yellow, green, and red, clasping the highly primed and energised Vajravarahi in red. The bell and thunderbolt, *ghanta* and *vajra,* representing a cosmic dyad, are the primary symbols and instruments of liberation—emptiness and form, wisdom and compassion, void and vibration, receptive insight (*prajna*) and skilful means (*upaya*). In the fusion and migration of deities between Hinduism and Buddhism, Chakrasamvara closely resembles Mahakala Shiva. Wrathful or ferocious deity-forms are a significant feature of Hindu–Buddhist iconography as *krodha-vighnantaka*s, "fierce destroyers of obstacles," to enlightenment and realisation.

Tantra literally means warp, weave, or loom. But it better connotes what has been described as "text, theory, system, method, instrument, technique or practice," a comprehensive technology for transformation at all levels, physical, emotional, mental, and spiritual.

Sadhguru Jaggi Vasudev famously said, "There is no Guru without a Tantra....Saints who are like gentle lilies and who bless people are beautiful in their own way, but they are not for people who are lusting for enlightenment. They are only for people who are just seeking small improvements in their life" (https://isha.sadhguru.org/in/en/wisdom/article/about-tantra-yoga).

[40] This public domain image is available at www.metmuseum.org/art/collection/search/78190

Diptych

Shiva Watches over Parvati Resting, c. 1780–90, Pahari Miniature

Jambhala or Kubera, the God of Wealth, 18th–19th century, gilded copper alloy, Trammell & Margaret Crow Collection of Asian Art, Dallas, Texas, USA

Literally, *yab–yum* means father–mother in Tibetan. The primal dyadic unity, the male–female energies that are the source of all creation, is symbolically represented in Hindu–Buddhist Himalayan art as an embrace between a male and female deity.[41] The image of Chakrasamvara and Vajravarahi is, in that sense, a yab–yum image. So is the figurine of Jambhala, with his consort, Vasundhara.

Between the male and female, this *yuganaddha,* the Pali word for harmonious yoking, congruence, and union, shows the interpenetration of wisdom and compassion.

That the idea was ancient and universal is evident in the Taoist conception of Yin–Yang. The two, male and female, father and mother, white and black, day and night, structure and fluidity, activity and passivity, and so on, together make the perfect whole, which is the essential nature of ultimate reality

The qualities that each embodies are meant to be neutral descriptors, not value judgements. Balance, mutuality, nurture, and interdependency is how the energies co-exist naturally.

Source: www.yinspiredyoga.com/blog/2018/1/30/yin-primer

[41] In the *Yoni Tantra*, Shiva, who has vanquished death, himself worships the Devi thus: "I am Mrityunjaya, beloved of your yoni. Surasundari, I always worship Durga in my heart lotus" (8). Indeed, he has become Mahadeva, the Great Lord, by worshipping and winning the favour of her generative power: "Listen Naganandini, by grace of your yoni I became Mahadeva! (20). —The *Yoni Tantra*, vol. 2, trans. Michael Magee (Harrow: Worldwide Tantra Project, 1995).

THE TRIŚŪLĀBJA-MANDALA OF THE TRIKA, PARĀ'S "THRONE"

From the opening verses of *Tantraloka* by Abhinavagupta:

Invocation of Parā (= svātantriya-śakti, icchā-śakti, and pratibhā)
naumi cit-pratibhāṃ devīṃ parāṃ bhairava-yoginīm |
mātṛ-māna-prameyāṃśa-śūlāmbuja-kṛtāspadām || 2 ||

I praise the Supreme Goddess [Parā Devī], the creative inspiration (pratibhā) of Consciousness, the yogic consort of Bhairava, who has made her abode the lotus-and-trident-throne, its prongs knower, knowing, and known. || 2 ||

Invocation of Aparā (= kriyā-śakti)
naumi devīṃ śarīra-sthāṃ nṛtyato bhairavākṛteḥ |
prāvṛṇ-megha-ghana-vyoma-vidyul-lekhā-vilāsinīm || 3 ||

I praise the Goddess in the body of the form of the dancing Bhairava, playful like a streak of lightning in a sky dark with monsoon clouds. || 3 ||

(Translation by Christopher Wallis "Hareesh": https://hareesh.org/blog/2015/7/31/light-on-tantra-tantrloka-11-21)

The Endless Love Tantra

Revealed by Paramesvara and Bhagavati in dialogic, energy exchange.

BHAGAVATI: My Lord!
For so you are to me.
So have I regarded you since the very beginning of time,
and so shall you be till creation reaches its culmination,
and all is known that is hidden,
and all is accomplished
that is still incomplete.
Since I am devoted to you alone,
please do reveal to me the secret of secrets.
How may I win your eternal favour and be united
with you forever? For truly, I seek nothing else.
Knowing my innermost desire, you must remove my distress.
Who else but you shall do this for me, Lord?

PARAMESVARA: My Beloved!
Adored, cherished, sublime spouse,
ruler of my heart, mistress of my soul,
my love, my destiny—dearest Devi Bhagavati!
Queen of all these worlds,
both below and above,
presiding deity of both the individual and collective
advancement in the here and hereafter,
prime mover, supreme energy, force, power!
Enabler and fulfiller of fates and fortunes,
Goddess supreme,
endowed with all the qualities of grace, beauty, and majesty,
bestower of boons and bounties,
yourself a bower of bliss...

BHAGAVATI: Enough, enough, My Lord.
Though I blush and beam to hear this litany of praise,
especially from your lips,
the question that absorbs and exercises me today
needs your urgent attention.
How to make permanent our sacred union:
that is the secret supreme that I wish to learn from you
without further delay.
Please, I pray, do not divert from the topic.
You must satisfy me today.

PARAMESVARA: You know that we have always
been together, since the very beginning of things,
and shall be thus until the very the end of time.
Realise that you are not apart from me
either in the now or in the hereafter.
All separation is an illusion,
perhaps a useful one, but ultimately untrue.
Why, then, do you speak as though we are not one?
Why, all of a sudden, such a question?

BHAGAVATI: It may be so to you, my Lord,
but to me, especially to the woman in me,
how it hurts—the idea of not being fully united
with you. Let me make a confession:
I long and crave for you in every human way
such that even a moment's separation is a torture.

I fear that I may lose you as
I have lost you so many times in the past.

PARAMESVARA: My Beloved,
I treasure and desire you too,
from life to life.
Then, why must you worry so?

BHAGAVATI: My Lord, allow me to explain.
Do you remember how I once asked you
about the garland of skulls you wear around your neck?

PARAMESVARA: Yes, my darling, I do.

BHAGAVATI: Do you remember
how at first you would not answer.
How you gazed into my eyes for an eternity
uttering not a word.
Then at length you said,
"Please do not misunderstand me, Beloved,
but such things must not be spoken of."

Those words hurt me.
I felt excluded from your secrets,
from matters you would not share with me.
Seeing the tears in my eyes,
you drew me close and tried to answer my question.

PARAMESVARA: Yes, of course I remember, sweetest.

BHAGAVATI: When I insisted,
you said, "Are you sure
you want to know?"
Then so abruptly and directly,
"My dear, these are the skulls
of all the women who have loved me."
I was shocked and almost recoiled from you.
Still you smiled at me serenely, unperturbed,
and gently pulled me close to you again.
There, nestling my head against your broad chest,
I thought, "What sort of man is this
who calls me his true love
even as he wears a garland of the skulls of all my rivals."

Divining my thoughts, for nothing is hidden from you,
you whispered the soothing words,
"Devi Bhagavati, my Beloved, I am ever true in love.
Those who love me I will never forget.
I keep loyal to them.
Those who have loved me even for one moment,
whosoever they be, I never abandon them.
And these—they loved and espoused me.
Because they are dead and gone,
does that mean I can overlook them?
They are still so close to me, close to my heart.
I do not give them up."

I shuddered and cried,
"But I want to be the only one you love,
the only one you ever loved, the only one in your life.
I pray you, throw those gory talismans away."

Again you smiled and said in soft and conciliatory tones,
"My dearest, truly, you have nothing at all to fear
or dislike in all these women who have loved me.
These are not trophies of previous conquests,
but abiding tokens of love and remembrance.
For their love was also true."

"As true as mine?" I blazed,

"I who have fasted and prayed and craved for you
like none other?
I who have performed such austerities for your favours
that even the earth trembled and the heavens
shook with fear?
How the very Gods came begging,
hands folded, pleading,
'Desist, desist from thy stubbornness.
The person you love can never belong to any woman,
not you, nor another.'

I scorned such sage advice;
I knew that one day the power of my devotion
would draw you to me.
And indeed it has,
which is why you are with me today.
Why, then, do you say,
that they have loved you too?"

You stroked my face tenderly,
even kissed away the tears springing from my eyes.
Gently, you replied,
"Who can match you in your penance and love?
You would have shaken off your very body
if I had not yielded to your insistence."

I felt comforted but I was not convinced.

I thought, "Why does he say so,
yet exalt all these women who also loved him?
Why does he not recognise
how singular and nonpareil my love is?"

I must remind you of our conversation that day
so that you take me fully into your confidence now.

PARAMESVARA: Oh, how sorry a figure I cut that day,
succumbing in love to you all over again!
BHAGAVATI: You, a sorry figure—*whoever*
has ever won an argument with you?
By silencing your own mind,
you still the thoughts racing through mine.
You are the Mahayogi, so words don't matter with you.

They cannot shake your poise.
I may rave and rant, but you never lose your temper.
If you did, the three worlds themselves would be destroyed
in the blazing, fiery gaze of your third eye.

PARAMESVARA: But, my dear, don't I always
willingly accept defeat at your hands?
Truly, I look forward to it.
I relish your victories.
Besides, if I were to get angry, really wrathful,
what would happen
to the three worlds and their denizens?
Your rage, too, would consume all
in its yawning maw.

BHAGAVATI: Who else, but I, can defeat you
—that is, indeed, true.
But only in love.
I defeat you in love, my Lord,
because I know how to love.
And as long as I love you as I do,
the three worlds and their inhabitants are all safe,
secure. For they are in my protection.

PARAMESVARA: "Bhagavati Devi!
Indeed, my strength comes only from you
and returns to you.

Even in your victory, it is I who win,
vanquished, conquered by your love.

Else, defeat and victory don't matter to me.
All is one.
All is as it should be.

BHAGAVATI: My Lord,
allow me to come back to that incident.

Do you not remember what you said?

PARAMESVARA: Beloved, I don't even remember myself
till you draw me out, reminding me of my nature.
My words to you are whisperings of your own heart.
For I am eternally and only yours.

BHAGAVATI: Ah! Well said, my Lord!
Your flattery makes me smile.
I am never tired of receiving your compliments.
But allow me to remind you of your own utterances.

"I know your mind, mistress of my heart,"
you said, "I know why you feel offended.
But believe me, it is without basis."

I replied, "How can it be without basis, my Lord,
when you imply that I am merely one
among the many who loved you?
I am not among the many.
I am the one, the *only* one."

You smiled,
"That you are, the only one,
the one and only.
Who could possibly deny that—
who *dare* deny that?"

"You jest with me, my Lord," said I,
pleased but also piqued, "Don't think
"I am so easy to appease as that.
What you have spoken is a contradiction.
Pray untangle it for me."

"How a contradiction, sweetest?"
you asked in mock earnest.

"Why, when you say many have loved you,
but then assert in the very next breath
that I am the one and only."

"Ah, therein lies the secret,"
you said softly,
"certainly, the secret of secrets."

"Deny it not to me," I cried,
"unclose your heart and tell it to me as it is."

"Very well, Devi,
listen then to what I say.
There is no contradiction because all these women
were only you, only forms and versions of you.
That is why I truly say that you are the only one,
that none has loved me but you."

Our conversation ended there.
I did not fully comprehend
your enigmatic pronouncement.
But you smiled and silenced your mind.
In its infinite hush, I, too, was drawn in.

I remember that pause,
or should I call it a sigh?
Silence, not solace—
that is what I would call it, my Lord.
But it would not, I resolved,
end here—this, our dialogue.

PARAMESVARA: True.
So it didn't, it hasn't ended there,
has it, Goddess?

BHAGAVATI: Of course not.
You know that I wasn't satisfied.
I desisted that time, but today I wish
to resume our unfinished conversation.

PARAMESVARA: Yes, Beloved,
I have been waiting
for you to do so.
I wonder if the time has come.

BHAGAVATI: Really?
I am surprised
and pleased to hear that.

PARAMESVARA: Do you think
I have not been preparing for this day
myself?

BHAGAVATI: Me too, Lord!
Truly, I cannot tarry any longer,
cannot bear further postponement,
but must be disabused at once
of my doubts and difficulties.
My soul cannot bear the rack of sharp discontent.
No more oscillating between hope and fear,
wanting you for myself but unable to secure you.

PARAMESVARA: Speak your mind openly,
my dearest. I am here to attend
to your every wish.

BHAGAVATI: My Lord, I have thought many times
on what you said.
Let me admit that at first
I did not believe you.
It was not that I lacked faith
in you or your words.
That can never be.
I love you and trust you implicitly.
But, in truth, what you said was puzzling.
How is it, I thought,
that the women who love you
come and go,
but you remain,
only you?

PARAMESVARA, *repeating softly, tenderly:*
How is it
that the women who love me
come and go,
but I remain,
only I?

BHAGAVATI: Could it be
that so many have come before me
and so many will come after?

PARAMESVARA, *again, repeating softly:*
Could it be

that so many have come before you
and so many will come after?

BHAGAVATI, *voice rising slightly:*
Then what of me?
Do I count for nothing?
Am I just another number,
one of the many pairs of ladies' slippers in your shoe rack?
We remove our shoes before we enter the sanctum.
There are rows upon rows of such pairs
of shoes outside the shrine,
but only one Shiva lingam inside.
Why this inequality?

PARAMESVARA, *repeating after her:*
Why this inequality?

BHAGAVATI: I found this not just hard to believe,
but harder to accept.
If this was truth,
it was very unpalatable.
Why was this the case?
There was only one Lord, but so many devotees,
so many Gopis, but just one Krishna.
Why? So, perhaps, I was one of many,
just one of your many devotees.

Before I could be disheartened or sad,
I remembered that you also said
that all those women were only me.
I felt a stab of joy.

Where was my jealousy then?
It was I, I alone, who had loved you from life to life.
I was the eternal woman in love again and again
with her eternal Lord.
I had taken all these births,
over and over, only to find you,
you, you, you, my Lord,
you alone have been the object of my desire and devotion,
eternally. Truly, I felt overwhelmed,
engulfed and brimming over with a mad ecstasy then.

To think that I alone sought you like this,
pursued you to every hideout of yours,
won you over and over again,
never ceased to be yours even in death,
assumed yet another body just to be with you,
no one else could love you like me;
you were meant for me and no one else.

That pleased me plenty.
I glowed with pride and certitude
as only a woman sure in her love can.
It seemed as if from that moment fear left me.
Why should I worry, why give myself to uncertainties?
Even if I fail this time, I shall surely find him again
—and again and again and again.
Indeed, I can *never* fail for my love is true
and exceeds the limits of my body.

My love is so great that it has dowered me
with inexhaustible bodies so that I can continue to love
my Lord. He is mine and only mine because
no matter how long he evades me,
so long shall I pursue him.

I felt happy and contented with that for many an age.

But then my dissatisfaction returned.

PARAMESVARA: Yes. Dissatisfaction returns.
That is the way. That is the truth.
After every temporary realisation, exultation,
the partial and limited self rebels.

BHAGAVATI: Why, why, why?
When will I find peace?
Lasting and abiding?
Today let me endeavour
to articulate my discontent again.
I must ask you something else,
something more, my Lord.

PARAMESVARA: Devi, most beloved and exalted,
ask, ask unhesitatingly.

BHAGAVATI: My Lord, let me accept what you say,
let me accept that you are right,
that life after life I have sought only you,
that the garland of skulls around your neck
is only composed of my own skulls
from my previous lives and bodies.

Let me also accept that you too have loved only me.
I alone have been the object of your desires,
drawing you out of your eternal aloneness
and self-absorption, spurring
you to create and animate these worlds,
and as many times again,
to destroy them,
drawing them back into yourself.

Yet, if this is true, my Lord, please tell me,
I beg you now, how is it that I alone take so many births,
go through so many lives,
changing so many bodies,
while you remain as you are?

Why am I born again and again
and not you?
Tell me that.
Why, oh why, do you alone
not have to undergo this punishment,
this constant separation and reunion?

PARAMESVARA: My own, the soul of my soul,
Devi dearest, you yourself know the answer
to these questions since it is your own *leela*,
endless play, ceaseless jouissance,
which has thus manifested
in the endless cycles of creation and dissolution.
Princess mine, queen and conqueror of every passion,
it is not that I am forever doomed
not to die, while you, condemned
to seek me from life to life,
must take birth over and over again.

No, it is not your lot to forget and remember
only seeking what you lost
in an inexhaustible, futile cycle,
from life to life.

Nor are you like any ordinary mortal
trapped in an unceasing cycle of samsara.

Process is pleasure to you, never punishment.
You delight in boundless and ceaseless creation.
You possess infinite variety, perpetual bounty.
You are the mother of plenitudes.
These worlds are made from and for your delight.

Thus have you enjoyed your many lives in as many bodies,
revelling in the ever-renewing recreation of elements,
the molecular dance, the hum of the universe.

BHAGAVATI: Vouchsafe to me, my Lord,
this secret, the secret of eternity.
For truly I am tired of this game and wish to end it now.

PARAMESVARA: You are tired of this game
but is the game tired of you?
The answer that you seek is yours
already to find.
But since you ask me thus,
let me reveal it to you once again:
we must assume countless bodies
till we know ourselves.

Knowing who you are,
you will never need to change bodies,
to lose and regain awareness.
Indeed, consciousness is unbroken
even if it seems intermittent.

BHAGAVATI: Ah! But suppose I want out,
to end this ceaseless cycle of samsara,
end it this very instant?

PARAMESVARA: The game is endless because
it too, like us, has no beginning and no end.
But we may stop playing it any time we like,
at least in the manner in which we have
been playing it since the beginning of time.
It's up to us what rules we play by,
the game's or ours.
For we created the game.
Why, then, should we allow the game to play us?

BHAGAVATI: You mean, we must stop
being played? No longer pawns
or even knights, rooks, or queen or king,
we must become
chess masters, grandmasters, wizards?
Do tell me how.

PARAMESVARA: Dearest, the secret eternal
is self-knowledge. When you know
who you are, false identification ceases.
Misidentification is the source of ignorance.
Ignorance causes rebirth, over and over again.

This keeps on happening in endless cycles.

Compulsive, unconscious, recurrent flows and patterns,
punctured by discontinuous flashes of awareness.

Once the latter steadies and stabilises,
the bouts of self-forgetfulness and remembering
become less frequent.

Then, suddenly, the illusion altogether drops
and you are fully awakened, fully attentive.

The minute you know your true self,
you will be free from the cycle of birth and death.

I remain the same while you change many bodies
because I know who I am
while you still forget, from time to time.

BHAGAVATI: I don't understand.
Is it so simple, this self-knowledge

that you speak of?

PARAMESVARA: If you think of yourself
merely as the body,
then you end
with the body.
But who is aware of the body?
Since the body cannot be aware
of itself, there must be awareness
apart from, albeit informing,

the body. If you know
yourself not as the body
which is the object of awareness
but as awareness itself,

then you will realise that
awareness does not need
a body, an object, apart
from itself. Awareness

does not cease to be aware,
cease to be, regardless
of body or object
because awareness remains

aware of itself. That, indeed,
is our daily experience. Do we
cease to be when we go to sleep,
forgetting our bodies?

If so, why not when our forms
change? As they must
from conception to birth,
childhood to adulthood,
thence to senescence
and old age,
finally to death?
No one remains the same.

We have changed so much,
so many times, time after time,
but persist in believing
that we are the same. Why?

Because it is our awareness
that has remained, persisted
despite and throughout
these changes. Even Gods

and Goddesses forget this,
sometimes, do not remember
who they are once they assume forms
and submit to incarnation.

But if we continue beyond
death as we know it, why
don't we remember? Why
the forgetfulness?

Actually, we do not forget.
Awareness never becomes forgetfulness.
It never forgets itself. Forgetfulness
comes and goes, awareness remains.

Those who know this become
aware even of their forgetfulness,
thus they regain awareness
the moment they seem to lose it.
I do not forget, as you can see.

I remember. From age to age,
life to life. Changing forms,
death and rebirth, time itself,

does not affect me. I am Mahakala,
the master of epochs, time-slayer.
I am consciousness itself,
without beginning or end.

Like a perennial stream
ever aware of itself,
eternal subjectivity.
No object contaminates

my freedom or limits
my being. I lack nothing,
I seek nothing,
I need nothing.

Knowing who I am
I experience no lack,
no incompleteness.
Thus I am ever myself.

You see me as you wish
or as you need to. By myself,
on my own, I have no form,
no name, no fixed identity—

or as many forms as you wish,
as many shapes or entities.
For they do not limit my singularity
or unity despite infinite diversity.

BHAGAVATI: Then who am I?

What is so difficult in knowing that?
I am the one who loves you.
You know that!

PARAMESVARA: True, true, my beloved.
But as long as you identify with this or that,
even the one who loves or is loved,
you will know coming and going,
birth and death.
You will change many bodies,
many forms, knowing both
the joys and sorrows of process.
Like the ladies whose heads
adorn my neck.
Identifying with the impermanent—
that is the door to death.
That is identity's last secret.

BHAGAVATI:
But without a body,
without a name and form
who loves whom?
How can one love that
which is insubstantial?
The secret still eludes me!

PARAMESVARA: Since you love only me
only pure awareness, knowledge
of the self, you too are bound
to discover the truth of your own identity
with yourself. That you too, despite myriad forms,
are nothing other than pure energy
pure awareness.

If you know that you are the gold

in each and every ornament,
no shape or figure limits you.
You remain gold no matter
which ornament or jewel you
choose to be shaped into.
You know you are the eternal gold
rather than the trinket form.
Goldness does not change,
only its appearances or forms do.
If your attachment is to this form or that—
whether yours or mine—
then what happens to "you"
when you shape-change?

When you cease to be the well-worn
Wedding band or signet ring
lost in the burbling brook
or gurgling stream?

If it is the ring that you seek
rather than the gold in the lost ornament,
won't you lose it again and again?

Eventually, you'll notice only goldness
in every adornment.
You will cease to be fooled or fixated
on shape or form.
You will desist from seeking or holding on to
any single object, shape, form, or body.

Aware yourself, you will only find
awareness everywhere,
aware of itself.

BHAGAVATI: No metamorphosis for me, my Lord.
I am attached to this form of yours.
Oh, I feel so incomplete without you as I know you now.
Why is that so?

PARAMESVARA: I don't believe you
for one minute. When all forms are yours
why would you prefer one to all the others?
If you do, it is only for the sake of convenience.

BHAGAVATI: Incompleteness, emptiness
—fullness, unity. These are two sides
of the same coin, so to speak,
aren't they, My Lord!
Emptied of myself,
I still remain myself;
myself added is still only me.

PARAMESVARA: Without you, I am still you.
There is nowhere where you
are not.

BHAGAVATI: Does this mean that I bring nothing to you
or you to me? Doesn't our love
count for anything in the here and hereafter?

PARAMESVARA: My fullness is enhanced by you.
The sun and its halo are one,
and yet they seem different.
The disc of the sun is too hot and bright
for the eye to see or bear.
But the halo of the sun softens somewhat
its glow. Similarly, the moon,
which I wear on my brow,
and the night which it inhabits, are one.
The moon is the gateway to the city of night.

But when the sun is eclipsed by the moon,
it still remains itself.
In you alone, in us both, or all by myself,
I remain who I am.
Myself.
There is none other.

BHAGAVATI: What then of our bond, our relationship?

PARAMESVARA: This bond of ours is indissoluble
and removal and addition of bodies
is only a figure of speech, not reality.
But knowing this full well,
you still seek me, find me, lose me,
then long for me, look for me, find me,
win me over, attain me,
then lose me all over again.
This is the play,
the interchange and intercourse
that you enjoy so well.

BHAGAVATI: Indeed, I do, Lord. I do so relish it.
But what about you? Do you not like it too?

PARAMESVARA: I neither look for you,
find you, nor having found you,
lose you, or forget you ever.
That is because I know myself.
In knowing myself I know you
because you are the being
of my innermost being.

BHAGAVATI: But, my Lord,
if I may press on,
shifting metaphors and crossing
traditions, among the endless Gopis
in the *raasamandala*,
only one surely does become, *is,* Radha?

PARAMESVARA: Radhe, Radhe, Jai Sri Radhe!
Yes, so she does, but every Gopi is potentially Radha.
Krishna multiplies himself endlessly
for each one's purpose and pleasure.

BHAGAVATI: My Lord, when Radha
cherishes, adores, worships
only Krishna. Then why,
O why, must Krishna consort
with so many Gopis?

PARAMESVARA: Each Gopi is only Radha.
Who else is she but Radha
in her manifold manifestation?

BHAGAVATI: Yet Radha desires her Krishna exclusively.

PARAMESVARA: Which is precisely why she sees so many rivals!

BHAGAVATI: What do you mean, my Lord?

PARAMESVARA: My Beloved, the illusion of multiplicity
is created by the desire for exclusivity.
In fact, it is only Krishna himself
who has become all these Gopis;
he alone becomes Radha
to enjoy himself.

For only Radha knows truly how to enjoy Krishna.
Thus Krishna must become Radha to know himself
in the way that only Radha can and does.

The Gopis think they enjoy Krishna,
but Krishna only enjoys *himself* in the Gopis.
It is only when Radha recognises this
that she becomes his real partner.

She becomes Krishna-maya,
nothing but Krishna.
Thus Radha Rani,
whom we adore,
is the Queen of Vrindavan.

BHAGAVATI: Radha is *in* love,
but Krishna *is* love.

PARAMESVARA: When desire is purified
it becomes love. Krishna has
no centre but exists in and of himself,
free of any body, like a body without organs or limbs,
indivisible, indissoluble love,
pure awareness.

Love discovers
itself over and over again in
and through those who seek it.

In the manner they love him, Krishna becomes theirs.

BHAGAVATI: To find love is to find you.
To the extent that love is yours,
I am yours too.

PARAMESVARA: I am wherever true love is.
There is no escape from me.
Wherever and whenever you have sought love,
you have only found and experienced some part of me,
some aspect of me.

BHAGAVATI: My Lord, please do not speak thus.
I cannot give you up.
It is because I love you
and want you to be mine forever
that I asked how to secure you in the first place.

PARAMESVARA: Fear not to lose me
you who have striven so hard to find me.

Do you not see in your own terrible form
you wear a garland of skulls too?

And a hold a cleaver dripping blood?
You step on my body lying supine underneath,

biting your tongue in mock-horror and
the self-restraint of not stepping on my chest

as you have half commenced to.
Look then at me.

My face is calm, eyes closed.
I am unconcerned.

Even if you kill me
in your mad and gory dance of death.

I too have sought you from life to life
till in the process I have found myself.

Brahman is the same as Maya,
Shiva the same as Shakti.

BHAGAVATI: Krishna and Kali, similarly,
are two facets of one truth, one and the same.

Smashana Kali (artist unknown)

This oleograph of the Goddess of the charnel ground represents the deity of annihilation. Her garland of skulls usually strings together 50 heads, representing each letter of the Devanagari alphabet. Hers is the dominion of the ultimate knowledge of life, death, and creation, represented by the interconnection of sound and sense, revealing the meaning and purpose of all things. Lying supine beneath her is Shiva, her consort, on whose chest her left foot rests.

Kali's skirt of arms represents her power to do, to act, and to control Karma. Her sharp sword of discrimination severs the stubborn skull of the ego.

"Kali," an oleograph by the Ravi Varma Press, Malavli, near Lonavala

Kali, the Terrifying Mother

Swami Vivekananda to Sister Nivedita: "Learn to recognise the Mother as instinctively in evil, terror, sorrow and annihilation, as in that which makes for sweetness and joy. Fools put a garland of flowers around Thy neck, O Mother, and then start back in terror and call Thee 'The Merciful'.... Meditate on death. Worship the Terrible. Only by the worship of the Terrible can the Terrible itself be overcome and Immortality gained....There could be bliss in torture too....The Mother Herself is Brahman. Even Her curse is blessing. The heart must become a cremation ground, pride, selfishness, desire, all burnt to ashes. Then, and then alone, will the Mother come!"

And the Englishwoman, shaken and bewildered by the storm, saw the good order and comfort of her Western faith disappearing in the typhoon of the Cosmos invoked by the Indian visionary. She wrote: "As he spoke, the underlying egoism of worship that is devoted to the kind God, to Providence, the consoling Divinity, without a heart for God in the earthquake, or God in the volcano, overwhelmed the listener. One saw that such worship was at bottom, as the Hindu, calls it, merely 'shop-keeping', and one realised the infinitely greater boldness and truth of the teaching that God manifests through evil as well as through good. One saw that the true attitude of mind and will, that are not to be baffled by the personal self, was in fact that determination, in the stern words of the Swami Vivekananda, 'to seek death, not life, to hurl oneself upon the sword's point, to become one with the Terrible for evermore!'"

—Romain Rolland, *The Life of Vivekananda and the Universal Gospel* (Almora: Advaita Ashram, 1931), pp. 164–165.

BHAGAVATI: Tell me, then, my own dearest,
should I stop loving you as a woman loves a man
so that I might love you as Supreme Consciousness?

PARAMESVARA: My most blessed and auspicious Devi,
make perfect your love,
whether human or divine,
for therein lies the secret,
the bridge between the human and the divine.
In fact, it is human love perfected, which is divine.

Love alone reconciles all differences,
melting the duality
between the woman and the Goddess,
between the lover and the beloved,
the object of love, the lover,
and love itself.

BHAGAVATI: But how,
is that possible, my Lord—
both human and divine
at the same time?

PARAMESVARA: There are two ends to love.
On one side the human, on the other the divine.
Love, like a rainbow, an umbilicus of grace,
unites the two. As you learn to love,
as you grow in love, you will find
the human slowly fusing with the divine
till they are one and indivisible,
inseparable, indistinguishable.

It is in the fullness of love that the human
loses itself and finds its own divinity.
Your very fears and anxieties
can propel you to higher truths and sacrifices.
Seeking perfect congruence, *yuganaddha*,
the highest union, when you yearn as a woman,
you will find yourself being loved back as a Goddess.

Only a man can make a woman feel like a Goddess.
By worshipping her. Gods cannot do so.
In their world, Gods are Gods,
Goddesses are Goddesses.
There is nothing special in being as you are.
But if an ordinary woman turns into a Goddess,
isn't that extraordinary?
That is what love, only human love, can do.

That is how human love becomes divine.
When your love becomes divine,
you will find the human loving you back,
which is what you long for, which is why
you ask me how you can continue
to love me like a woman loves a man,
even though you are a Goddess, not a mortal.

Radha is the apotheosis of human love.
Her love leads her to Krishna, the Divine Beloved.
When her love transforms her into God's paramour,
God himself starts to love her back
as an ordinary human being would,
adoring her, pleasuring her. She dresses up—
and undresses—for him. He presses her feet,
serves her, humbling himself before her.
Though he is the King of Mathura,
he forgets not only his *rajamaryada*,
his divine prestige and prerogative,
but even his *devamaryada*,
the etiquettes and constraints

enjoined upon him as a God.
The humble milkmaid
of Vrindavan becomes the queen of his heart.
Vrindavan becomes the sacred grove
where even the Gods long to sport,
but cannot enter because it is the exclusive preserve
of human beings, the devotees of the Lord,
his *sakhas* and *sakhis,* dearer to him
than the denizens of heaven.

BHAGAVATI: My gracious Lord,
tell me, then, what love perfected is.
Rather, *show* me, please.

PARAMESVARA: My lovely lady,
perfect love is endless love.
It is the path as well as the destination,
the here as well as well as the hereafter.

Endless love is the consecration
of everything as an offering to love.
Live in love, live for love, breathe love, exhale love.
Empty your heart of all but love.

I have nothing but love, am nothing but love.
I have relinquished everything else.
I have nothing to offer but love.
I seek nothing but love.

I am penniless except in the currency of love,
naked except in the garb of love,
homeless except for the shelter of love.
Love is my refuge, love is my treasure,
love my sole offering, love my sole demand.
I come in love, I seek nothing but love.
In love is my ruin, in love my fulfilment.
In love is my return.

Love is my beginning and my end.
Love is my destination and my destiny.
If I fail, let me fail in love,
let love also be my saving grace.

Love turns every failure on its path
into a resounding success.
Love is my humility, love is also my pride.
Love is my joy, love my surrender.

I come armed with love,
I am also utterly disarmed by love.
I offer only love, I ask only for love.
I live for love, I die for love.

BHAGAVATI: Thus if I approach you,
my Lord, surely, I will find that you are mine in love
as I am yours.
From here unto eternity.

PARAMESVARA: Endless love, then,
is path and destination,
human and divine,
fallible and perfect.
Indeed, love is all there is.
In love there is neither you nor me.
BHAGAVATI: Or both of us finding ourselves in each other.

PARAMESVARA: Not knowing where one ends
and the other begins.

BHAGAVATI: The combination

of *vairagya* and *alingana*,
detachment in attachment.

PARAMESVARA: The simplest union
and simply the best.

BHAGAVATI: My Lord, I can only thank you
for showing me the way to your heart,
which is also the way to mine own.
Thus having secured you,
I hope to enjoy you
forever in leisure and pleasure,
as the very heart of your heart,
the soul of your soul,
such as is enunciated
only in in this,
our Endless Love Tantra.

PARAMESVARA: My sweetheart, may all women
who aspire to be the perfect soul-companions
to their chosen mates follow your path of endless love.
Therein will they find peace and fulfilment.
May those who desire the things of this world
as well as the higher bliss of heavens
tread softly on this path of endless love.

It is the way to unite the human with the divine,
the physical with the metaphysical,
the natural with the supernatural.

But it is only for those who can
walk the difficult and narrow,
thorny and stony way of love.
It is not for those who just seek
their own gratification or are merely needy
or greedy for worldly happiness.

For this is the path not of gratification
but of renunciation.
It is purely in giving up the separate self
that one attains the unitive existence.
Love is nothing but ceaseless sacrifice,
the continuous offering of the self
as libation to the fire of purification and truth.

Love is the friction that creates the fervour of transformation.
Love is also the cooling rain dousing the fire of passion,
affording the pleasure of release
by tempering the rasping choler of craving
with the fragrant unguent of compassion.

This Tantra of Endless Love
is also the be-all and end-all for men in love.
It is the guide to all men who return love with truth.
The two, love and truth, are identical.

Together, let the happy lovers,
consonant and content
regarding us as the chosen deities of their ritual,
contemplate us:
Parvati and Paramesvara.

BHAGAVATI: My Supreme Beloved,
embodiment of Bliss-Consciousness-Truth,
my one true Love and Lord,
may we always come thus together
in this Tantra of Endless Love
that we have manifested together.

PARAMESVARA: Yes, my lovely Queen,
whose single, careless, side-long glance
liberates millions of toilers,
from the grind-wheel of samsara,
in your satisfaction lies my heart's peace.

Thus may this Tantra of Endless Love,
as bountiful as the milk
of knowledge, kindness, and kinship
in your bounteous breasts, nurse and comfort
mortals restless for *Srividya,*
the auspicious intelligence
which alone can free both desperate souls,
and famished ghouls, and other creatures galore,
inhabiting the three worlds,
waiting for your mercy to release them.

BHAGAVATI: You remain pristine, invincible, singular,
Svyambhu, self-manifesting,
Yogi supreme,
and *Sakshin,*
ultimate witness.
Not one of a dyad,
not one pole of a binary,
but complete, indivisible, eternal in yourself.
That is why I turn to you,
over and over again,
for in truth I know
that only you can satisfy my quest for attaining my very self.

PARAMESVARA: This day,
on Mahashivaratri,
having revealed
my true nature to you,
Beloved Devi, is also the auspicious hour
when we shall be united forever.
You will know no more birth and death,
no more comings and goings.

BHAGAVATI: How so, Lord?

PARAMESVARA: Henceforth, we shall never be parted.
You will inhabit half my body.
Together, we shall be one body,
male-female at once,
cohabiting and conjoint
for ever.

So saying, the Lord vacated half of his body for his beloved Bhagavati. In every temple in India, they are worshiped thus, inseparably together, *yoni* and *lingam*, Shakti and Shiva, and when shown more explicitly, in the androgynous form of the *Ardhanarisvara.*

Namo Parvati Pataye Hara Hara Hara Mahadeva!

This superb miniature, artist unknown, circa 1820, probably comes from Kangra, Himachal Pradesh. Painted in opaque water colours and gold on paper, about 9 x 6.5 inches, it depicts the merged entity, Shiva-Shakti, with their at-peace mounts, Nandi, in the left background, and the tiger, in the front right, curled up, eyes closed.

Ardhanarishvara and the Descent of the Ganges, Gift of Mr and Mrs Lessing J. Rosenwald, 1959, Philadelphia Museum of Art

Epithalamium

The painting suggesting the mood of mutuality and harmonious reciprocity is a Pahari miniature from Himachal Pradesh. Shiva and Parvati share a tender moment in a landscape which is peaceful but full of quiet enchantments. Parvati, eyes closed, is in restful repose her head on Shiva's lap, as the latter, reclining over her, contemplates her with his protective and loving gaze.

Parvati's right hand, safeguarding her stomach, makes us wonder if she is expectant.

In the front, a benign Nandi, Shiva's vehicle, looks on peaceably, head slightly lowered, giving the couple both privacy and support.

Once identity's last secret is revealed, there is no loss, no craving for return, no separation.

What was once the open wound is now the passage to never-ending union.

Seeing Light in the Night

At the sacred shrine,
prone on the ground face down,
he is overwhelmed.

Unequal to the torrent of grace
descending upon him,
slaking his timeless thirst.

So longed for, now undeniably real—
Goddess! How irresistible is thy favour,
how benign thy gaze!

The cold stone of the slate floor
is scalded with his hot tears.
He doesn't feel like lifting himself up.

Has he found,
after so many wasted lifetimes
and wrecked opportunities,

the true purpose of life,
the principle of bliss,
the mantra to end separation and suffering?

Right in front of him,
two Goddesses.
One resplendent in her turmeric *sringara,*

shining in splendour
in her sanctum sanctorum,
she blesses all with equal encouragement.

The other, *sarvagunasampanna,*
endowed with befitting qualities,
now stands beside him.

As if in answer to a silent prayer,
she now turns towards him,
with a full waist's arched longing.

Even more delectable in profile,
she smiles slightly.
He hasn't been surer of benificience.

Now she touches his hand lightly
to share in his offerings
on the flaming plate of the aarati.

The Goddess in the shrine,
she who births and sustains the cosmos,
and the one by his side,

who assumes the form
of individual companion and saviour—
are they one and the same?

Which one shall he adore?
The Sara of Samsara
or the Sarva of Brahmanda?

Today, it seems,
both are benevolent:
he has no need to choose.

At night,
again the air throbs with fullness
and swell.

She lowers her eyes,
as she unfastens the clasp,
like peeling fruit.

Suddenly, two doves
aflutter,
spring free.

A shiver of terrible delight
runs up his spine.
When face to face,

the colour rises
up her cheeks.
to the tips of her eyes.

She looks at him.
Words and touch just yet
seem unnecessary.

In pristine
bemusement,
her collar bones shimmer.

Then the gift
underneath throbs,
an audacious curvature,

first dipping smoothly,
then pointing upward as if
in urgent challenge.

Two taut syllables,
like bursting buds,
stare at him accusingly.

Such opulence
can no longer be disregarded
or denied its due.

He reaches out and touches her.
To his tentative entreaty,
an incantation flowers

in a slow miraculous motion.
At last he utters the secret invocation:
OM Tat Savitur Varennyam!

Afterword

I

A book such as *Identity's Last Secret* cannot be written overnight. Or even over several nights. Though one might burn the proverbial midnight oil in its composition, intensification, and revision.

At its core, *Identity's Last Secret* is about a difficult relationship and its aftermath. But to decipher the riddle of such a relationship is no less a challenge than fathoming the enigma of life itself. And, quite graphically, *dramatically,* it is a blood trail that leads back to the original wounding. That is also the path to the surcease of pain and, eventually, the mastery of suffering.

Which is why this book has stayed with me, urgently and insistently, for the good part of the preceding decade. Not only did the writing of it generate insights and modifications in my life, but also secured changes in the real world. The book could not be published till these transitions resulted in a decisive turn in my world.

Like the answer of the universe to a plea or prayer.

More than ever, the writing of this book has convinced me of the power of the word. Can there be any doubt that the word moves and alters reality? Contrary to W.H. Auden's pessimistic dismissal, "Poetry makes nothing happen," the word can be life-changing if not earth-shattering. Like a mantra, the energised word, through its very utterance, whether voiced or silent, sends a reverberation across the cosmos.

As to changing our own minds, many have experienced, *experimented with,* what writing can do. Words come to us from mysterious sources. By invoking, nurturing, formulating, and releasing them, we can modify our circumstances and shift our consciousness.

Writing can be both therapeutic and dynamic. It can heal us and mend hearts. That is because much of our world is actually of our own making. We only think that external forces control our lives.

In realising ourselves, we change our relationship with others and, in fact, with the universe too. Poetry, thus, the writing and reading of it, can fundamentally modify our perception both of ourselves and the world.

II

Systems of Yoga and Tantra are predicated on the profound knowledge of the causative forces of life. The supreme drive which also makes us scatter or consciously pass on our genes to the next generation some call sexuality, others Love. It enables us to continue to live in our progeny and descendants, endowing us with a sense of our continuance.

But what if instead of just genes, we could transfer and transmit our energies in the form of enchanted and forceful words? Thereby activating and operationalising our *ichha sakti, gyan sakti,* and *kriya sakti*—the power of will, knowledge, and action?

The ancient Indian praxis of alchemy, Tantra, employed our fleshly vulnerabilities and susceptibilities to trigger and accelerate such a modification and mutation. They used the power of our sexual vitality, our reproductive energy, not only for procreation or recreation, but for transformation.

Identity's Last Secret, similarly, tries to combine poetry with eroticism, literary criticism, philosophy, spiritual exegesis, and visual culture to prove, as it were, its own purpose. In an attempt to instantiate the aspired-for transmutation in both mind and material reality.

The physical, thus, turns trans-physical. Emotional trauma may thus find itself transfigured into eustress and eudaimonia. Finally, the mind ends up facilitating its own sublimation in mystic metamorphosis. An unconventional or unprecedented mix? Sri Aurobindo said, "Poetry rather determines its own form; the form is not imposed on it by any law mechanical or external to it."[*]

In such a book, the visual, not just in the diagrams and paintings, but also in the shape, form, and arrangement of the lines, is very much a part of the intended design. The whole book is a *yantra,* a device, engine, appliance of word and image calculated to readjust one's awareness.

In so doing, it integrates the major movements and preoccupations of my own intellectual and creative endeavours over the past 40 years. This is a book of a lifetime as far as I am concerned.

Sri Aurobindo observed that poetry, at its highest, is nothing short of "the discovery of the word, the divine movement, the form of thought proper to the reality" or more succinctly, poetry is the "mantra of the Real" (ibid 10).

[*] *The Future Poetry*, vol 26, *Collected Works of Sri Aurobindo* (Pondicherry: Sri Aurobindo Ashram, 1997) p. 13.

Naturally, *Identity's Last Secret* makes unusual, if not exceptional, demands on its readers too. Not a simple, breezy read, to be leafed through casually or lackadaisically, I would like to believe that it is nothing less than the book of life.

III

Yet, *Identity's Last Secret* is a work of imagination. All its characters are fictional, even if they read and refer to real texts and authors. In the integrity of writing or purity of the word, it nonetheless seeks to honour truth, albeit poetic, rather than factual.

From the abstract to the concrete, however, there may be much slippage and misprision. We see, not only in our society, but in many parts of the world, that unpleasant facts are the enemies of political correctness. In art, however, telling truths is paramount, though the truths of art are quite different from those of practical reality.

Even so, for lines which, for whatsoever reason, give offence to whichsoever section of my readers, I offer my sincere regrets. The purpose of this book cannot be to cause insult or affront. On the contrary, it is an effort at catharsis, penance, purification, and realisation.

It is impossible to fix the meaning of words, let alone prevent them from being construed differently from how they were meant. Such misapprehension is what makes literature so challenging, so full of possibilities. For such are our lived realities and how they turn into literature.

Identity's Last Secret is a homage to woman, who according to the Tantras, is matrix of creative energies of the cosmos. The myriad combinations of the masculine-feminine, whose polarities manifest even in same sex love, constitute the veritable building blocks of the manifest universe.

Very often, as both writers and human beings, we gloss over difficult relationships which belong to our several pasts. Instead, we might consider each of them a sacred match rather than a proverbial battle of the sexes. Both in the sense of pairing and contest, we can live and learn as we work our way through them.

Even if some do not work out in the end.

To rewrite or deny the past for contemporary compulsions is not the way out. There is no reason to disown those we loved. Our muses, even those unnamed or maimed, nurtured us and our wor(l)ds. Our gratitude to them, both personal and artistic, is perennial.

Love makes us lose our minds. Love also returns us to sanity.

Art cannot dodge karma, but it helps us go beyond it.

IV

In writing *Identity's Last Secret*, I have incurred many debts. The first of these is to my spouse and partner, Gayatri, to whom the book is dedicated. Finding her was nothing short of the realisation of a life-changing mantra. She has also contributed the sketches in the book, except those which have been identified otherwise.

Dr Pariksith Singh, medical practitioner, entrepreneur, humanist, poet, mystic, savant, creative prodigy, was instrumental in pushing *Identity's Last Secret* to its present shape and form. He also wrote its extremely generous Foreword. My book belongs to the earliest batch of BluOne Ink, his new publishing venture. I thank him and his entire team, especially Partho Sanyal and Geetanjali, Anirudh Chakravartty and Mugdha, and Pankaj Singh and his ferociously creative RED colleagues, Seepiya and Garima.

We know, across multiple domains of human endeavour, that content is not everything. Sometimes it is not even enough. Design and delivery make the difference. In a successful artefact, form, function, and aesthetics fuse into one purpose.

When it comes to *Identity's Last Secret,* I wish to thank Deepika Mehta, the book's gifted designer. Deepika's collaboration and friendship have raised the book to a new level of aesthetic realisation. I believe, the final product is truly a verbal and visual treat, a celebration.

This book was written in spurts, read out at literary meets, and revised in various parts of the world—Singapore, Tübingen, London, New Delhi, Bengaluru, Jaipur, Goa, Colombo, Maldives, Hanoi, Austin, and Shimla, among others. To the friends, colleagues, not to mention the air, water, and soil of these locations, I offer my gratitude and respect.

Finally, my unending appreciation to those who cared to read the manuscript and offer words of support or encouragement.

—Makarand R. Paranjape

Identity's Last Secret

"There are two ends to love. On one side the human, on the other the divine. Love like a rainbow, an umbilicus of grace, unites the two," says Makarand R. Paranjape in this audacious, multi-textured volume that fuses poetry, philosophy, art, and literary criticism into a genre-warping modern Tantra of longing and fulfilment.

Identity's Last Secret is Makarand's most ambitious work of what may be called poetic art. Interweaving poetry, philosophy, criticism, visual art, and even a modern Tantra, it tries to tease out answers to our most profound self-questioning and suffering.

A darkly turbulent relationship, characterised by instability and emotional violence, ends in abandonment. Obsessive, almost addictive, passion leaves a wound whose identity must be revealed before healing and wholeness can be reclaimed.

But the answer lies not in the aesthetics and politics of postcolonial translation, but in the blood trail that leads back to the gash. A never-healing wound is the double-bind of both art and life.

The solution to our existential puzzle is not the regaining of lost love. The wound marks us, but we are not marred by it. It is how we are bound to the Beloved. It is our way back. We are the wounded. We are also the blessed: "Identity's last secret/ could never be known—or even if known, it could never be told:/ he was not merely loved, he was beloved—and he was not alone."

Once identity's last secret is revealed, there is no return, no separation. The open wound is the passage to never-ending union. When Shiva turns half his body into the Goddess, they are always one, the supreme symbol not just of androgyny but of non-dualism.

Makarand is the author or editor of over fifty books. His academic papers, book chapters, and journal publications number over 175. He is also the author of thousands of columns, op-eds essays, reviews, and other popular publications, published in newspapers, magazines, and online media portals.

His creative work includes six books of poems, two novels, a collection of short stories. His last book of poetry was Transit Passenger (Passagerio em Transito), an Indo-Brazilian volume of verse published by the University of Sao Paolo Press.

"I saw the mythic retelling more as a human acknowledgement of confusion and failure, as a renewed pledge, tattered but resilient, to confront the terror and uncertainty of living a life 'utterly disarmed by love.'"

- Arundhati Subramaniam on Identity's Last Secret